INCLUSION:
A Service, Not A Place

A WHOLE SCHOOL APPROACH

Alan Gartner, Ph.D.
Co-Director,
National Center on Educational Restructuring and Inclusion (NCERI)
The Graduate School and University Center
The City University of New York
New York

Dorothy Kerzner Lipsky, Ph.D.
Director,
National Center on Educational Restructuring and Inclusion (NCERI)
The Graduate School and University Center
The City University of New York
New York

PUBLISHING

A Division of
National Professional Resources, Inc.
Port Chester, New York

JAY

Gartner, Alan
    Inclusion: a service, not a place—a whole school
    approach/ Alan Gartner, Dorothy Kerzner Lipsky.—1st ed.
    p. cm
    ISBN 1-887943-54-4

Inclusive education—United States
Mainstreaming in education—United States
Handicapped Children—Education—United States
Classroom management—United States
Educational change—United States   I. Lipsky, Dorothy Kerzner
II. Title

LC1201.G37 2001   371.9'046
    QBI01-701035

Cover design by Faith Deegan
Book design by David Gates Creative, Tucson, AZ
Production by Alice Bowman, The Service Bureau, Tucson, AZ

© 2002

Dude Publishing
A Division of National Professional Resources, INC.
25 South Regent Street
Port Chester, NY 10573
1-800-453-7461
1-914-937-9327 Fax

Visit our Web site: *www.nprinc.com*

DEDICATION

For our children and grandchildren!

Table of Contents

1

Introduction and Overview

This book is designed both to accompany the video, "INCLUSION: A Service, Not A Place—A Whole School Approach," and to serve as a hands-on, free-standing implementation resource for teachers, general and special education, and other school personnel. It may be used by teachers in their classrooms and/or as an integral part of the school or district professional development activities. While focusing on the work of those general and special education teachers who provide instruction, the book supports the roles of administrators, clinical personnel, and parents.

It presents a "how-to" guide for implementing a whole school approach to inclusion, emphasizing the changes in the roles and activities of *all* school personnel. While the book is grounded in the education of students with disabilities and their inclusion in the regular education environment, it is designed to support the work of all teachers who have a diverse student population in their classroom.

To facilitate the use of materials compiled/developed by the authors, fourteen Blackline Masters (BLMs) are provided. These may be reproduced and used for classroom and/or staff development purposes. These BLMs are located at the end of the chapter in which they are referenced. Each reference includes the number of the BLM; e.g., BLM No. 4, and the page where it is located. These BLMs are contained within a heavy black border.

The material in the book builds upon the activities of the National Center on Educational Restructuring and Inclusion (NCERI) in its work with school districts, urban, suburban, and rural, and state education agencies across the country. NCERI's work includes professional development for school and administrative personnel to support the implementation of inclusion, research about inclusion "best practices" and the effects of its implementation, and dissemination and publication of material. The book derives from the experience of more than a thousand school districts throughout the nation. It draws upon the growing body of "best practices" that have been identified by practitioners and researchers.

In today's schools, diversity is manifested in all aspects of demography: race, ethnicity, religion, language, economics, sexual orientation, family situation, and student transiency, as well as disability. At issue for schools and classrooms is not the reality of difference, but what we make of it. As a nation, we are moving from glorification of the melting pot to an honoring of the mosaic. Or as Minow (1990) has said in discussing the "dilemma of difference," the shift no longer "makes the trait [or disability] signify stigma or isolation but responds to the trait as an issue for the entire community" (p. 84).

The book begins with discussion of the reauthorized Individuals with Disabilities Education Act, P.L. 105-17 (IDEA), particularly the mandate for "whole school" approaches. It then provides a "how-to" approach to the development of a program (IEP) for students with disabilities, and spells out the requirements for the education of such students. It helps teachers design programs that provide the mandated access to the general curriculum, and it gives information on the implementation in the classroom of supplementary aids and services and participation in state- and district-wide assessments. In addition, the book provides a guide for regular education teachers to participate effectively in the development of the student's program.

The book supports the implementation of inclusive practices by presenting the following:

- a definition and description of the inclusive practice,
- the relationship of the practice to IDEA,
- "best practices," based upon experience and current research,
- roles for school personnel, administrators, related services providers, and clinicians,
- roles for parents,
- "black line" masters for use in staff development activities, or by teachers to help structure inclusive classrooms,
- references for additional treatment about each topic,
- additional information about resources, organizations, videos, Web sites, and
- a glossary.

Where can I find additional information (research, policy data) about inclusive education?

There is an ever-growing body of books, articles, and handbooks that document the research, policy, and data issues about inclusive education. They include the following:

Armstrong, F. & Barton, L. (Eds.) (1999). *Disability, human rights and education: Cross-cultural perspectives*. Buckingham, UK: Open University Press.

Bauer, A. M. & Shea, T. M. (1999). *Inclusion 101: How to teach all learners*. Baltimore, MD: Paul H. Brookes Publishing Co.

Daniels, H. & Garner, P. (Eds.) (1999). *Inclusive education*, 2nd edition. World Yearbook of Education, 1999. London: Kogan Page Ltd.

Lipsky, D. K. & Gartner, A. (1989). *Beyond separate education: Quality education for all.* Baltimore, MD: Paul H. Brookes Publishing Co.

Lipsky, D. K. & Gartner, A. (1997). *Inclusion and school reform: Transforming America's classrooms.* Baltimore, MD: Paul H. Brookes Publishing Co.

Lombardi, T. P. (Ed.) (1999). *Inclusion: Policy and practice.* Bloomington, IN: Phi Delta Kappa Educational Foundation.

Lupart, J., McKeough, A., & C. Yewchuck (Eds.) (1995). *Schools in transition: Rethinking regular & special education.* Toronto, Canada.

Stainback, W. & Stainback, S. (Eds.) (1990). *Support networks for inclusive schooling: Interdependent integrated education.* Baltimore, MD: Paul H. Brookes Publishing Co.

Villa, R. A. & Thousand, J. S. (Eds.) (2000). *Restructuring for caring and effective education: Piecing the puzzle together.* Baltimore, MD: Paul H. Brookes Publishing Co.

Vitello, S. J. & Mithaug, D. E. (Eds.) (1998). *Inclusive schooling: National and International Perspectives.* Mahwah, NJ: Lawrence Erlbaum Associates.

The Special Education Resource Center (SERC) has prepared several useful bibliographies, including *Integration/Inclusive Education for Students with Disabilities*; *Curriculum and Instructional Adaptations in the Mainstream*; *Disability Awareness, Integration and Inclusion*; and *Children's and Adolescents' Literature on Disability Awareness, Integration, and Inclusion.* SERC, 25 Industrial Park Road, Middletown, CT 06457. (860) 632-1485.

Books that focus on particular aspects of implementing inclusive education are listed in subsequent chapters. They include the following:

Algozzine, B., Ysseldyke, J., & Elliott, J. (1997). *Strategies and tactics for effective instruction*, 2nd ed. Longmont, CO: Sopris West.

Capper, C. A., Frattura, E. & Keyes, M. W. (2000). *Meeting the needs of students of ALL abilities: How leaders go beyond inclusion.* Thousand Oaks, CA: Corwin Press, Inc.

Giangreco, M. F. (1998). *Quick guides to inclusion 2: Ideas for educating students with disabilities.* Baltimore, MD: Paul H. Brookes Publishing Co.

Halvorsen, A. T. & Neary, T. (2001). *Building inclusive schools: Tools and strategies for success.* Boston, MA: Allyn and Bacon.

Hammeken, P. A. (2000). *Inclusion: 450 strategies for success: A practical guide for all educators who teach students with disabilities.* Minnetonka, MN: Peytral Publications.

Index for inclusion: Developing learning and participation in schools. (2000). Bristol, UK: Centre for Studies on Inclusive Education.

Kochhar, C. A. & West, L. W. (1996). *Handbook for successful inclusion.* Gaithersburg, MD: An Aspen Publication.

Reif, S. F. & Heimburge, J. A. (1996). *How to reach & teach all students in the inclusive classroom.* West Nyack, NY: The Center for Applied Research in Education.

There is a growing body of data concerning the outcomes of inclusive education practices. They include the following:

Freeman, S. F. N. & Alkin, M. C. (January/February 2000), "Academic and social attainments of children with mental retardation in general education and special education settings," *Remedial and Special Education*, 21(1), 13–18.

Lipsky, D. K. & Gartner, A. (Spring, 1995), "The evaluation of inclusive education programs," *NCERI Bulletin*, 2 (2), 1–7.

MacGregor, G. & Vogelsburg, R. T. (1998). *Inclusive schooling practices: Pedagogical and research foundations. A synthesis of the literature that informs best practices about inclusive schooling.* Baltimore, MD: Paul H. Brookes Publishing Co.

National study of inclusive education, 2nd edition (1995). New York: National Center on Educational Restructuring and Inclusion, The Graduate School and University Center, The City University of New York.

Staub, D. (September/October, 1996), "On inclusion and the other kids: Here's what research shows so far about inclusion effects on nondisabled students," *Learning Magazine*.

Staub, D. & Peck, C. A. (December 1994/January 1995), "What are the outcomes for nondisabled students?" *Educational Leadership*, 36–39.

2

(IDEA) P.L. 105-17
"Individuals with Disabilities Education Act"

Just for the fun of it: Test your knowledge of IDEA.

What are the major provisions of the law?

_____

_____

Turn to page 6 to read about this topic.

What does the law say about students with disabilities and the regular curriculum?

_____

_____

Turn to page 7 to read about this topic.

What is the meaning of the concept of understanding special education as service not a place?

_____

_____

Turn to page 8 to read about this topic.

What does the law say about service in the general education environment?

_____

_____

Turn to page 9 to read about this topic.

What is a "whole school" approach? How is this manifested in the school? What are the steps in developing a "whole school" approach? How can such an approach be assessed?

_____

_____

Turn to page 14 to read about this topic.

What are the features of an effective school?

_____

_____

Turn to page 18 to read about this topic.

What are general education interventions?

_____

_____

Turn to page 20 to read about this topic.

What does the law require?

The essential feature of the 1997 reauthorized IDEA is the requirement that a student with disabilities be involved and progress in the general curriculum. The law defines the "general curriculum" as that curriculum which each state has designed for its students in general.

To achieve this goal, the law mandates the following:

- enhanced content of the Individualized Education Program (IEP),
- inclusion as the norm unless there is specific justification for a student not to participate with nondisabled students in academic, extracurricular, and nonacademic activities,
- provision of supplementary aids and services,
- involvement of a regular education teacher at the student's grade level in the development of the IEP,
- professional development for regular and special education personnel involved in providing services for students with disabilities,
- state funding formulas that are "placement neutral": ones that do not promote or encourage placement of students in more restrictive settings, and
- students with disabilities to participate in general state- and district-wide assessments, with needed accommodations and modifications.

According to this law, the education program for students with disabilities must:

- address the general curriculum, not a separate special curriculum,
- provide the program in the regular education classroom, where the general curriculum is the norm, unless otherwise justified,
- identify the needed supports to enable the student to make progress in the general curriculum,
- be designed by a team including someone familiar with the general curriculum, e.g., a regular education teacher at the child's grade level, who is to be provided professional development to play this role,

- be funded by the state in a design that does not encourage separate services,
- assess student learning per the general state- and district-wide program, with needed accommodations and modifications for the individual student.

IDEA's requirement is that students with disabilities have beneficial access to the general curriculum. The law defines the "general curriculum" as that required by each state for students in general education. The requirement is mandated regardless of the student's placement. Those who provide instruction in either general or special education settings must know the general curriculum. Several provisions of the law address engaging students with disabilities in the general curriculum. The following are three important factors:

- *The IEP*: In the development, review, and revision of a student's program (i.e., the IEP), a regular education teacher at the student's grade level must participate with the other members of the IEP Team. (This is to be the case for all but a few students, where a prior decision, reached with the parents' involvement, has been made that the student will not participate in the regular education environment.)
- *Personnel:* All personnel involved in the student's education, regular education teachers and special education staff, teachers and related services providers, must be informed of their responsibility to implement the student's IEP and the specific accommodations, modifications, and supports that must be provided for the student;
- *Resources:* Funds are available to school districts to provide professional development to regular education teachers in serving students with disabilities.

The IEP is the primary tool[1]
The IEP is the primary tool for ensuring the student's involvement and progress in the general curriculum. To achieve this, the IEP must:

- *Describe the present level of performance:* This includes how the student's disability effects her/his involvement in the general curriculum. The presence of a disability is not warrant alone for exclusion from such involvement;
- *Specify measurable goals:* The student's progress in the general curriculum must be measured, at least annually, against a set of clearly defined, measurable goals;
- *Identify services:* The student's special education and related services, and supplementary aids and services needed to support involvement and progress in the general curriculum, are to be identified; and

- *Specify supports for school personnel:* The student's program must specify the supports which enable school personnel to promote student progress in the general curriculum and participation in extracurricular and nonacademic activities.

The presumption of an inclusive environment

Since the passage of P.L. 94-142's, "Education for All Handicapped Children Act", in 1975, the Least Restrictive Environment (LRE) concept has been a part of the federal law. Neither the term "inclusive education" nor the word "inclusion" appears in the law; however, education of a student with disabilities with her/his nondisabled peers is the presumption, unless specifically rebutted. Special education is considered a service, not a physical place.

The reauthorized IDEA sharpens the provisions of previous laws by requiring that in the development of a student's IEP there must be specific justification of a decision for a student not to participate with nondisabled peers in academic, extracurricular, and nonacademic activities. This justification must be particularized, subject area by subject area, and involves all of the activities of the school, the entire academic curriculum, clubs, sports, after-school activities, and student transportation. Prior to proposing exclusion, the IEP Team must have considered the benefits of related services and modifications or supports for the student and/or school personnel. "IEP Team" is the term that the federal government uses for the group that determines whether a student is disabled, based upon IDEA's specification of twelve categories of disability,[2] and in need of special education services. If the student is in need of special education services, the IEP Team then develops the program of services. Members may vary from state to state, as does the name of the team; for example, some states use the term "Committee on Special Education," others "Child Study Team," and still others, different terms. This book uses IEP Team as the generic term.

Provision of supplementary aids and services (SAS)

The term supplementary aids and services, specified in the law, is often confusing to teachers and administrators, as they initiate a "whole school approach" to inclusion.

"Supplementary aids and services" for a student *and* her/his teacher(s) are the tools or help that is needed to enable students with disabilities to gain benefit from their involvement with the general curriculum. The focus in this book is on the provision of supplementary aids and services to support a student's participation in academic activities. Equally, the law requires the provision of such aids and services to support a student's participation in nonacademic and extracurricular activities. This includes all clubs and after-school sports and activities. The law and its requirement regarding supplementary aids and services applies to all of the activities conducted by the school district; it is in effect, 24 hours a day, 7 days a week. Illustrative of the range of this effort is the following report: "Around the country, an increasing number of educators argue that school districts should provide more integrated transportation for students with special education programs."[3] The report notes that "school districts have started using innovative methods to conquer what some call the final frontier for 'inclusion': the bus ride."[4] These methods include equipping some full-size buses with wheelchair lifts, pairing students with disabilities and nondisabled students to ride on the bus together, having aides ride the inclusive regular bus, and using all sized buses for all groups of students. Also suggested is including bus drivers at meetings that craft a student's program.

For the most part, the supports used by teachers in regular classrooms for students with disabilities are appropriate for all students. With this being the case, the supports that teachers find successful for students without disabilities make the participation of the student with disabilities more natural. One of the most common statements made by teachers in inclusive classrooms is that, "Good teaching is good teaching is good teaching."

Among the range of supports that teachers report as most effective in an inclusive classroom are the following:

- collaborative teaming and consultation,
- team teaching,
- curriculum adaptations,
- environmental accommodations,
- building friendships,
- cooperative learning,
- classwide peer support activities,
- inclusion facilitators,
- heterogeneous grouping for instruction,
- study skill training,
- use of technology, and
- alternative instructional strategies (e.g., differentiated instruction, multi-sensory instruction, small group instruction, heterogeneous grouping for instruction).

In deciding among these supports, teachers will want to consider the extent to which the support can:

- maximize student participation and interaction,
- enhance the respect and dignity of the student,

- promote independence,
- build on the learner's strengths,
- increase the student's self-esteem,
- be generalized across school and community settings, and
- benefit all students.

Regular education teacher participation in IEP development

Historically, a student's IEP had been developed by special educators, including both evaluative and pedagogic personnel. In the reauthorized IDEA, Congress has recognized the importance of the participation of a regular education teacher at the student's grade level in the development of the student's IEP. As the goal is the student's involvement and progress in the general curriculum, it becomes essential that someone familiar with that general curriculum be involved in the design of the student's program. The only exception to this requirement is if a prior decision has been made that the student will not be served in the general education environment. School districts are increasingly recognizing that such an important decision should be made as part of the IEP development and not prior to it, and are including a regular education teacher as a matter of routine. This process supports a school district, should litigation be brought by parents at a future time.

While the requirement of the regular educator presents scheduling issues for schools, his/her presence has several important benefits. These include:

- ensuring that the IEP addresses the actual content of the grade's general curriculum,
- offering the opportunity for the regular education teacher to identify the supplementary aids and services that are needed to support the student's progress in the general curriculum, and
- providing the opportunity for the teacher to identify the supports s/he might need in order to enable the student to make progress.

As to this last point, the IEP Team meeting presents a unique opportunity for a regular education teacher to have her/his professional development needs addressed. Should a support be recommended for a student by the IEP Team and the teacher not be familiar with it, then the teacher may request professional development to learn the new skill/practice, or support by a specialist, such as a psychologist, social worker, reading specialist, or another teacher. For example, should a behavior management program be required for a student, the classroom teacher can request assistance in developing and implementing a behavior plan. As part of a student's IEP, providing support to a teacher becomes an obligation of the school district.

Professional development for general education personnel

The reauthorized IDEA replaces the model of students with disabilities receiving services only in special education classes from "special educators." Instead, given the goal of involvement and progress in the general curriculum, regular education personnel are to be integrally involved in the education of most students with disabilities, both in the program design and its implementation. Each of a student's teachers and other service providers, special and general education, must be informed of their role in implementing the student's IEP, including the specific accommodations, modifications, and supports that must be provided. The rules concerning confidentiality of student records do not preclude the informing of all school personnel involved in a student's program, nor is ignorance of the provisions of the IEP a basis for failure to implement it.

In recognition of the training needs of all staff, the law authorizes the use of IDEA personnel preparation funds to support the professional development of general education personnel. The law requires that each school district disseminate information on promising educational practices to all staff, including general and special education teachers, support staff, and administrators. In addition, the law requires that districts adopt such promising practices.

"Placement neutral" funding

Prior to the passage of the 1997 IDEA amendments, the Congress found that in nearly all of the states the funding of local school districts for special education services encouraged more restrictive placement; at the same time the law required services in less restrictive settings. While the percentage of state funding for local districts varies from state to state, the national average of state funds provided is about fifty percent of the local cost of special education.

The reauthorized IDEA now requires each state to establish a "placement neutral" funding formula that does not encourage more restrictive placements. As IDEA's funding increases over the years, the new funding will be allocated based upon the overall number of students in a school district (sometimes called "census-based" funding), rather than the current system that provides a "bounty" for labeling students.

It is expected that this change in state funding formulas, along with the changed basis for new funding, will encourage school districts to sustain students in general education settings rather than place them in more restrictive special education settings. The funding changes can provide more "prevention" services for *all* students in general education without requiring a special education label prior to the intervention. Based on this shift in the federal law and state practices, many schools are now providing services within general education that had previously been defined as special education. These services may include speech/language services as well as counseling, and physical and occupational therapy. Providing services in a more natural setting for all students and offering the opportunity for these services without children being labeled can be a great benefit for the whole school. For the school district, it means eliminating expenses in conducting unneeded evaluations and having additional funds to provide a greater extent of "prevention" services.

In the reauthorized IDEA, services provided to students with disabilities may also benefit nondisabled students; this is a consequence of the revocation of the "incidental benefits" rule. For example, effective instructional design and feedback procedures as part of an individualized behavioral intervention plan for a given student with a disability may have benefit for the class as a whole. The provision of IEP-prescribed resources or related services in the general education classroom, sometimes called "push-in" services, may serve to benefit all students, including those who are not disabled.

Participation in state- and district-wide assessments

Since the goal for students with disabilities is involvement and progress in the general curriculum, the law provides for assessing the learning of students with disabilities through general state- and district-wide assessments. For about five to fifteen percent of students with disabilities, the Congress held that the regular assessment, even with modifications, would not be appropriate. For these students, an alternate assessment is to be used. Each state was required to develop an alternate assessment no later than July, 2000.

The supplementary aids and services in instruction are to be provided to enable the student to make progress in the general curriculum and should be parallel to the accommodations and modifications that are to be provided in the assessment process. Such accommodations and modifications are not to be limited solely to district- and state-wide assessments; they are to be integrated into classroom instruction. The implementation of supplementary aids and services in instruction and accommodations and modifications in assessment enable a student to demonstrate her/his knowledge to the classroom teacher, and provides the student with familiarity with the accommodation and modification, when it is used on the district- and state-wide assessment.

Accommodations and modifications are designed to enable students with disabilities to demonstrate what they know; this minimizes the influence of the impairment on the outcome to be measured. One can conceptualize three types of accommodations and modifications as related to assessment:

- mode of assessment, e.g., extra time given for the student to complete the test, a different location for the test,

- format of the question, e.g., use of Braille rather than printed text, larger print, reworded questions, questions on tape or read to the student, and

- format of the answer, e.g., use of other than a "bubble" answer sheet, answers dictated or recorded.

The federal requirement does not specify the precise nature of the accommodations and modifications to be provided for students with disabilities. As states and districts implement this requirement, issues of test reliability and validity are being raised. As "high stakes" tests are increasingly used to determine grade-to-grade promotion and high school graduation, the application of accommodations and modifications only for students with disabilities presents a set of concerns about standards and validity.

In what was characterized as "a major victory for disability rights groups," the Educational Testing Service (ETS) in early 2001 has decided to stop noting on the scores sent to colleges that students with disabilities took standardized tests with special accommodations, such as extra time.[5] The ETS decision came as settlement of a California case, filed by a man with no hands, who was granted extra time and the use of a computer with a trackball for taking the management test. The policy, which will cover the Graduate Record Examination, the Graduate Management Admission Test, the Test of English as a Second Language, and Praxis (a test for teachers), eventually could have much broader effect, as it covers tests for precollegiate education.[6] Pointing to the broader consequence of the decision, a Disability Rights Education and Defense Fund (DREDF) lawyer, who represented the plaintiff, pointed out that, "If you don't have time restraints, you don't have the problem with accommodations."[7]

The reauthorized IDEA asserts that for students with disabilities schools set "high expectations and ensure their success in the general curriculum." In measuring the progress of students with disabilities, it is the student's learning that is to be the focus, not the manifestation of the disability.

IDEA requires that the results of these assessments are to be made public and provided to parents, with the same detail and frequency that the district provides for reporting the assessment of nondisabled students. The Congress emphasized that students with disabilities are to be treated as a regular part of the school community. As this practice, based on the IDEA requirement, has been implemented across the country it has enhanced accountability for the learning of all students.

What is a "whole school" approach?

The importance of a "whole school" approach is expressed by the Congress in the reauthorized IDEA. The law says that the education of students with disabilities will not be enhanced by "tinkering" with special education; rather, what is called for is a systematic and systemic approach. The school as a whole is expected to be a place where special education services are provided, and these services are to be provided in the context of the school as a unit. Special education is no longer to be considered a place to which students are sent; it is a service or group of services which students receive, across all activities of the school. Providing services to students with disabilities in the general education environment increases the likelihood that "prevention" or enhancement can be provided to nondisabled students without labels.

The "whole school" approach incorporated in IDEA is consonant with the provisions of the Comprehensive School Reform Demonstration (CSRD) program, established by the Congress in 1997, the same year that IDEA was reauthorized. CSRD provides funds for a school-by-school approach to educational reform. Between 1998 and 2000, more than eighteen hundred schools received CSRD funds. (Funding for subsequent years has been increased.) The "whole school" approach of IDEA ensures that as schools adopt one or another research-based model per CSRD, the reform is directed to benefit all students, in an inclusive design.

Central to the changes in IDEA is the expectation that intervention must begin before a student fails. The basic "whole school" approach involves strengthening the overall educational program, so that all classrooms provide a basis for effectively educating a wider range of students. In a school characterized by an inclusive education approach, there will be:

- MORE experiential, inductive, hands-on learning,
- MORE active learning,
- MORE emphasis on higher order thinking and learning of key concepts and principles of a subject,
- MORE in depth study of a smaller number of topics,
- MORE responsibility transferred to students for their own learning,
- MORE choice for students,
- MORE enhancing and modeling of the principles of democracy,
- MORE attention to affective needs and the varying cognitive styles/intelligences of the students,
- MORE cooperative, collaborative activity, among both students and teachers,

- MORE heterogeneously grouped classrooms, where individual needs are met,
- MORE provision of help in the regular class setting,
- MORE varied and cooperative roles for teachers, parents, administrators, and community members, and
- MORE reliance upon teacher descriptive evaluation of student growth.

At the same time, there will be:
- LESS whole-class, teacher-directed instruction,
- LESS student passivity,
- LESS classroom time devoted to fill-in-the-blank worksheets, dittos, workbooks,
- LESS teacher focus on "covering" large amounts of material in every subject area,
- LESS rote memorization of factors and details,
- LESS stress on competition and grades,
- LESS "tracking" or leveling of students in "ability groups,"
- LESS use of pull-out programs, and
- LESS use and reliance upon standardized tests.[8]

Schools across the country have developed a variety of general education intervention formats, involving groups of general and special educators, and using such terms as "Teacher Assistance Teams," "Pupil Personnel Committees," "Child Study Teams," etc. Regardless of the name or the particular composition of the group, the goal and purpose of the effort is to marshal the full range of the school's resources, and to provide services to the students and the teachers in the general education environment. To attain greater success for students and teachers, schools need to use "best practices" and to create an on-going problem-solving environment that engages the full range of resources.

The BLMs Nos. 1, 2, and 3, pages 23–24, 25–26, and 27 may be used in a whole school approach to inclusive education, to determine goals, attitudes, and professional development needs.

How to get started with a "whole school" approach?

Inclusive schools and school districts are at different places implementing a "whole school" approach that incorporates special education as a service in general education. While the federal law provides the framework within which all schools and districts must operate, there are many variations in how schools initiated the changes. According to the NCERI national study of greater than a thousand school districts, these include: a school board decision, an administrative directive, teacher initiative, parent discussion or court case, and a university (or other)-funded project. Regardless of the initiation point, school districts have identified four common successful activities in the implementation process. They need not be used in a tightly prescribed sequence but can be viewed as key activities in developing a "whole school" approach to inclusive education. More information on these four activities follows.

1. Develop a district policy and a school mission statement

The "whole school" approach presented in the reauthorized IDEA suggests that a district policy concerning inclusion, and a school mission statement, should not be free-standing documents. They should be developed consistent with the practice of the district/school and be viewed as a part of the district and school overall design. If the practice in the district is for policies to be developed by a board of education committee that includes members of the community, a similar practice should be followed here. If the development of a school mission statement involves administrators, teachers, and parents, that should be the practice followed for this activity.

2. Inform parents and community

Parents and other community members need to be informed about IDEA and consequent school changes, and they need to become actively engaged at the school level. The overall tone in describing the inclusive education program should be in keeping with the school/district's approach to informing parents and community of any other change, as in the introduction of a new curriculum, a new grade organization, etc.

While there are separate program and placement issues that require the necessary involvement of parents of students with disabilities as part of the IEP process in regard to their child(ren), parents of nondisabled students also need to have information about the school/district policy and changes in the school mission and activities. The first general parent meeting should be convened by the principal, with other staff participation as appropriate. Among the topics for the meeting(s) are the following:

- explanation of the background for the change,
- its grounding in federal and state law, as well as district policy,
- the experience nationally and locally that demonstrates benefits for all students, disabled and nondisabled, and
- description of the steps and schedule of implementation at the school.

Written material to supplement the oral presentation should be available. Pilot efforts in the school or district can be presented by teachers and parents, and often are an effective method for transmitting information. Opportunities to visit programs, in the district or nearby, or to see a video should be made available.

The Blackline Master No. 4, page 28, "Questions That Parents Often Ask," may be completed by the school/district and then used at meetings for both parents of general and special education students.

Responses to the following questions can shape the work of the Planning Group:

a. Why have students been referred for special education services in the past year?

b. What is the design of the current special education program?

c. What practices/procedures in general education support/inhibit an inclusive school environment?

d. Which students presently served in more restrictive settings would benefit from special education services provided in the general education classroom, with needed supplementary aids and services?

e. What are the professional development needs of the school staff?

3. Establish a school planning group

Prior to the initiation of any significant program change, all groups in the school should be represented in the planning process. This includes: general and special educators, classroom personnel at the various grade levels/subject areas, related services and other support personnel, administrators, and parents. If the school already has a school leadership team, or similar group, that is widely representative, it would be appropriate to use (or build upon) this organization.

While it is not essential that the principal be the chair of the group or participate on a meeting-by-meeting basis, it is essential that the school leader is active and supportive. Additionally, it should be made clear that the planning will have a direct effect on the entire school and is not a special education activity. For those not directly involved in the work of the planning group, arrangements should be made to keep the staff regularly informed of the group's activities and progress.

4. School Self-Assessment

The initial work of the planning group is to conduct a school self-assessment. After the data is collected and analyzed, the planning group should move to developing a school plan and timeline for implementation.

Questions for the Planning Group: Developing a "Whole School" Approach
The following questions can serve as a guide for the school self-assessment.

a. *Why have students been referred for special education services in the past year?*

In examining referrals for special education or of students "at risk" and served without a special education referral, a cluster of needs is likely to emerge. In the NCERI study, districts across the country reported that referrals clustered in three groups: failures in reading and mathematics instruction, issues of discipline and student behavior, and matters of student family and home life. Often appearing were clusters at particular grade levels, especially at grade three or four, when the curriculum became more complex and/or external testing began. The purpose of the referral analysis is to determine what additional (or alternative) resources and programs could be established in general education to support students and enable them to remain and succeed in the regular classroom. The analysis is *not* to preclude students from receiving special education services, when needed. Rather, its purpose is to identify which broad services and programs are needed in general education and which become a part of the basic school program to reduce the need for special education referrals and services.

b. *What is the design of the current special education program?*

Examining the design and organization of the school's current special education services and program makes it possible to identify how services are organized, the number of students served in special education classrooms (i.e., outside of the general education setting), in general education classrooms, and the staffing of those classrooms. To serve all of a district's students in their home school, the school which they would attend were they not identified as having a disability, would move a district toward natural proportions of students, disabled and nondisabled. This would enable students to attend school with their siblings, friends, and neighbors. The personnel staffing special education classes as well as out-of-classroom personnel represent resources for the planning group to consider as they explore the (re)deployment of staff to enable the school to provide needed supports for students with disabilities in regular education classrooms. Collaborative teaching or other models of classroom support are discussed in Chapters 4 and 5.

c. *What practices/procedures in general education support/inhibit an inclusive school environment?*

In examining school practices, the separation between general and special education programs and services may emerge and will warrant examination. Whatever their appropriateness in the context of a separate special and general education system, separate practices may inhibit the development of a unitary system. Different student registration procedures, separate rosters, differing procedures for ordering of texts and other materials, separate evaluation of pedagogic personnel, are each examples of practices that reflect separation and mitigate against an inclusive school environment.

The Blackline Master No. 5, pages 29–30, "School Self-Assessment: Practices in General Education that Support or Inhibit an Inclusive School," can be used to develop a comprehensive school plan.

d. *Which students presently served in more restrictive settings would benefit from special education services provided in the general education classroom with needed supplementary aids and services?*

Teachers in self-contained classes and others knowledgeable about the students in restrictive settings should review each student to identify what supports could be provided in general education classrooms. This is the first step in a process that will culminate in the IEP Team, including the parent, considering a change of placement.

Teachers of general education inclusive classes surveyed in the NCERI study report that their students, disabled and nondisabled, are more alike than different. They report that on standard outcome measures, the scores of students with disabilities would more likely be distributed than to be clustered at the lowest level. This finding should encourage an expansive approach to the consideration of students for participation in the general education classroom. In keeping with the ethos of IDEA, this consideration should be undertaken focusing not on the student's disabilities nor on how s/he would perform in the class as it is currently conducted; rather, the consideration should be based upon how the student could perform with needed supplementary aids and services.

e. *What are the professional development needs of the school staff?*

The needs of staff for professional development will vary, by role as well as prior training and experience. In the needs assessment phase of developing the school plan, it is important to be specific and to offer teachers the opportunity to identify their professional development needs without fear of being labeled as incompetent. Some teachers may want to learn more about alternative instructional strategies or curricular modifications and others may want to learn more about the content of the general curriculum. And the process of collaboration may need to be learned by all staff. Clinical personnel may want to learn strategies for working in classrooms, with students and in support of teachers. Related services providers may want to learn about how to integrate their services within the regular classroom program.

While some professional development needs will be common across some or all of the schools in a district or among all staff in a particular role; in such instances, district-level professional development activities may be warranted. For the most part, however, professional development should be building-specific. In conducting professional development activities an underutilized resource is the expertise of the members of the school staff. The practice of teachers observing training and/or mentoring has been demonstrated to be very effective. In a team teaching model, professional development takes place between the collaborators. When two teachers with areas of expertise work together and share their knowledge, the outcomes are positive for both professionals. (See Chapter 4.)

The Blackline Master No. 6, page 31, "Professional Development: A Self-Assessment Guide," may be useful.

5. The school plan

The plan should provide the basis for the school to become a quality inclusive school, where for the most part services for students with disabilities are provided in general education classrooms. The design of a whole school approach to the education of students with disabilities is the culmination of the self-assessment activities, data collection, and its analysis. The planning group should avoid what has been called the "paralysis of analysis." In general, several months is sufficient time to conduct the school self-assessment and develop a building plan to present to the school staff and parents.

The plan should be specific and include a time frame for the implementation of its components. It should address:

- specifics of students to be served in the new inclusive program options,
- profile of staff to serve students in the new design(s),
- program models to be used,
- organizational and scheduling changes that are necessary,
- professional development activities needed,
- process and methods for evaluating program and student outcomes.

The process of adopting the plan will vary district-by-district. Whatever the particular procedures, this process should include sharing with parents and community, informing the entire school staff, and determining the consequences of the proposed changes on school-district relationships.

The Blackline Master No. 7, page 32, "School Plan: Issues to Consider," may be used to develop the whole school approach.

6. Evaluating outcomes

A school must develop a way to assess and measure the outcomes of the implementation of the building's plan, and to use it to provide the basis for ongoing change.

Along with standard measures of student outcomes, the school planning group should address how they will measure the following issues:

- what are the effects for all students, in academic, behavioral, and social areas?

- what are effects for all staff in terms of enhanced school capacity; this includes staff professional development, new organizational models/ practices, (re)deployment of personnel, and classroom practices?

- What are the numbers of students previously served in special education classrooms in or outside of the home school building that now are being served in the home school? In general education classes with needed supports?

The Blackline Master No. 8, pages 33–35, "Quality Indicators of an Inclusive Environment," based upon NCERI's work with school districts across the country, as well as a review of the research literature, can be initially used in a number of ways: in the planning process, and later as a review of progress made and as a monitor of implementation.

Where can I find additional information on IDEA?

The basic source of information is the law itself, Public Law 105-17. It can be found in most public libraries and also is available from the Office of Special Education Programs (OSEP), US Department of Educations, Washington, DC 20202. The other official document is the regulations, published in the *Federal Register*, March 12, 1999.

Each state has a federally-funded Parent Training and Information Center (PTIC), which provides material for parents and others about the law. The PTICs can be contacted through the special education unit of each state education department.

Many professional organizations provide material concerning the law. The two largest are the Council for Exceptional Children (CEC) and TASH. (See Chapter 9 for a list of organizations.)

Perhaps the most comprehensive resource on this topic is "Discover IDEA CD 2000." This CD-ROM provides information on policy and practices related to IDEA, including:

- statute PL 105-17,

- final regulations,

- analysis of comments from *Federal Register*,

- topic briefs on critical issues,

- over 400 presentation slides,

- over 50 policy and practice publications,

- contact information for federally funded assistance projects.

See *www.ideapractices.org* or e-mail *ideapractices@CEC.Sped.org*.

Regarding "whole school" approaches and the restructuring that is required, Lipsky and Gartner (1997) and Villa and Thousand (2000) offer good general descriptions, while Halvorsen and Neary (2001) provides helpful guidance and work materials (e.g., district- and building-level assessment and planning materials). Capper, Frattura and Keyes (2000) provides a well-structured planning process.

EFFECTIVE TEACHING PRACTICES: A SELF STUDY GUIDE

School practice and research findings report that for classrooms to be effective teaching and learning environments, they must address the lesson and classroom issues. The following presents examples of "best practices." Looking at your teaching practices, give an example of how you have used any of the following:

Lesson—

• A focus on district/state standards.

_____

_____

• Content, materials, and resources that are appropriate to the needs of *each* student.

_____

_____

• Clear expectations, connecting this learning experience to previous learning.

_____

_____

• Models, guided practice, and varied opportunities for students to demonstrate mastery.

_____

_____

• Ongoing assessment opportunities, including specific criteria for success.

_____

_____

• Opportunities for students to work with and support one another.

_____

_____

• Meaningful extensions, applications, and homework assignments.

_____

_____

Classroom—

• Posted examples of students' work, both in progress and completed.

_____

_____

(continued on next page)

- A library of high-interest books, at different reading levels, available for students to use as resources and to read at home and in school.

  _____

  _____

- A variety of resources to use in projects, classroom instruction, and activities.

  _____

  _____

- Displayed information that reflects the students' backgrounds (reflecting diversity in terms of race, gender, culture, language, disability, and sexuality), and interests.

  _____

  _____

- Models, rubrics, and other information that assist students in their learning.

  _____

  _____

- Technology to support student learning, including higher order activities.

  _____

  _____

- Daily and weekly classroom schedules, highlighting any changes to the normal routines.

  _____

  _____

The classroom as a positive learning environment—

- Posted classroom and school rules and procedures.

  _____

  _____

- Clear expectations regarding appropriate student participation and behavior.

  _____

  _____

- A clear hierarchy of positive and negative consequences for various behaviors.

  _____

  _____

- Guidance and instruction in appropriate behavior.

  _____

  _____

Inclusion: A Service, Not A Place, by Alan Gartner & Dorothy Kerzner Lipsky

FEATURES OF AN EFFECTIVE SCHOOL: A SCHOOL STUDY GUIDE

School practice and research findings report that for schools to be effective teaching and learning environments, they must address schoolwide issues of curriculum, instruction, and staffing. The following presents examples of "best practices." For your school, give an example of:

• How the school instructional program is developed in the context of standards and assessment, which incorporate a range of curricula offerings and a variety of instructional strategies.

_____

_____

_____

• Alignment of curriculum, instruction, and assessment.

_____

_____

_____

• Staff diversity, and the provision of professional development and support.

_____

_____

_____

• Collaboration among school staff.

_____

_____

_____

• Programs of student empowerment, including peer learning programs, active learning opportunities, and student-to-student support activities.

_____

_____

_____

• Family and community involvement in the school.

_____

_____

_____

• Access to community and agency services, to serve students and to support school staff.

_____

_____

_____

(continued on next page)

- Schoolwide approach to behavioral issues, with shared expectations, standards, and consequences across all settings.

  _____

  _____

  _____

- Presence of a regular system of accountability that defines success by the learning of each and all students.

  _____

  _____

  _____

- A system of transitional supports from school level or setting to new level or setting.

  _____

  _____

  _____

- Ongoing assessment and evaluation of student learning in the context of identified schoolwide goals.

  _____

  _____

  _____

- Program of general education supports or interventions* that address student needs in the regular education setting.

  _____

  _____

  _____

*The term "general education supports or interventions" is preferred to the more commonly used terms of "pre-referral," which suggests that this is a necessary step prior to a special education referral, or "prevention," which suggests that special education may be some sort of a disease.

Inclusion: A Service, Not A Place, by Alan Gartner & Dorothy Kerzner Lipsky

QUESTIONS FOR TEACHERS: GENERAL EDUCATION INTERVENTIONS

Interventions in the general education program make the classroom a more effective learning environment for a wider range of students. Identify and give an example of:

- Modified classroom structure or physical arrangement.

_____

_____

- Changed physical layout of the classroom.

_____

_____

- Changed student classroom assignment from my to another general education class.

_____

_____

- Adapted curriculum.

_____

_____

- Used alternative curricula approaches and/or instructional strategies.

_____

_____

- Used classroom positive behavior support program.

_____

_____

- Used specialist services to support whole class learning. (e.g., reading or literacy specialists, guidance counselors, remedial specialists, related services personnel, nurse or other health services providers)

_____

_____

- Fostered needed services of parents of the students in my class.

_____

_____

- Used supports provided in the general education class per the IEP of a student with disabilities being made available, as appropriate, to nondisabled students.

_____

_____

Inclusion: A Service, Not A Place, by Alan Gartner & Dorothy Kerzner Lipsky

---

QUESTIONS THAT PARENTS OFTEN ASK

- What are the education reasons for the district/school offering a different model of services/ programs for students with a disability? _____

- What does the federal law (the reauthorized IDEA) say? What does it require of our district? Of our school? _____

- What has been the district's experience in implementing IDEA? What has been the experience elsewhere in the state? The nation? _____

- What are the steps toward implementing IDEA? How will staff be prepared? How will outcomes be assessed? How will parents be informed of the outcomes? _____

- Will my rights as a parent be the same? _____

- Will the changes benefit students with disabilities at the expense of nondisabled students? _____

- Will including students with disabilities in regular classrooms overwhelm the teacher? Water down the curriculum? Slow up the learning of other students? _____

- Will the nondisabled students learn inappropriate behaviors? _____

- Will students with disabilities be able to obtain the special services they require in regular classes? _____

- Will children with disabilities be teased? Ostracized? _____

- What will happen to the staff, general and special education? _____

- How will the parents of children with disabilities relate to the additional school staff serving their children? _____

- Will the district's/school's budget be impacted? _____

- Will confidentiality be ensured? _____

Inclusion: A Service, Not A Place, by Alan Gartner & Dorothy Kerzner Lipsky

---

SCHOOL SELF-ASSESSMENT GUIDE:
PRACTICES IN GENERAL EDUCATION THAT SUPPORT OR
INHIBIT AN INCLUSIVE SCHOOL

Whatever the appropriateness of particular school organizational and administrative practices in the context of a separate special and general education system, such practices may inhibit the development of a unitary system. For each of the following, consider the general practice and then address whether there are differences between special education students/staff and general education students/staff. If so, consider the rationale and continued appropriateness of such differences.

- How are registers set?

  General education: _____

  Special education: _____

- What are class size limitations?

  General education: _____

  Special education: _____

- How are student/teacher schedules set? For core subjects? For specials?

  General education: _____

  Special education: _____

- How are funds allocated?

  General education: _____

  Special education: _____

- How are other resources (e.g., textbooks, workbooks, computers, supplies, etc.) allocated?

  General education: _____

  Special education: _____

- What are reporting lines?

  General education: _____

  Special education: _____

- What are the lunchroom practices, e.g., location and time?

  General education: _____

  Special education: _____

(continued on next page)

- What are the patterns of supervision?

  General education: _____

  Special education: _____

- How is classroom space allocated? Other facilities?

  General education: _____

  Special education: _____

- How is pedagogic staff assigned? Support personnel?

  General education: _____

  Special education: _____

- What are the school hours?

  General education: _____

  Special education: _____

- When does the school day begin/end ?

  General education: _____

  Special education: _____

- What are the practices regarding extracurricular activities? Is transportation available? Are needed adaptations provided?

  General education: _____

  Special education: _____

- Are parents of all students eligible for membership in the school's parent-teacher organization(s)? To hold office?

  General education: _____

  Special education: _____

Inclusion: A Service, Not A Place, by Alan Gartner and Dorothy Kerzner Lipsky.

PROFESSIONAL DEVELOPMENT:
A SELF-ASSESSMENT GUIDE

This questionnaire is part of our school self-assessment and is being used to identify professional development needs. The following are important practices in an effective classroom with general and special education students. Please identify areas of professional development which you feel would strengthen your classroom and our school. Also, please identify areas where you can offer assistance or training.

Check as many as apply

Classroom Practice	I would like professional development in this area	I can offer professional development in this area
Alternative assessment		
Alternative instructional strategies		
Assessment accommodations & modifications		
Assistive technology		
Collaboration		
Collaborative instructional planning		
Cooperative learning		
Curricular adaptation		
Differentiated instruction		
Multi-media instruction		
Paraprofessionals in the classroom		
Peer support programs		
Positive behavior support		
Preparation of general education teachers to participate in IEP meetings		
Provision of related services into classroom instruction		
Social integration/skill development		
Student self-management		
Study/test taking skills		
Supplementary aids & services		
Teaching/learning strategies		
Team teaching		

Name (Optional) _____

Inclusion: A Service, Not A Place, by Alan Gartner and Dorothy Kerzner Lipsky.

SCHOOL PLAN:
ISSUES TO CONSIDER

There are many components of a school plan that promote inclusive education. In the context of districtwide policies, your school plan should address the following components:

- a philosophy that articulates the rights and abilities of all students to learn and to belong,

- the full school staff sharing responsibility for meeting the needs of all students in each class,

- teachers, general and special, dividing responsibilities in a collaborative design,

- teachers having time to discuss and plan ongoing instructional activities,

- support personnel being in the classroom for a long enough period of time and on a consistent enough basis for them to collaborate effectively,

- the school using natural proportions in the classroom, and home school placements for students with disabilities,

- classroom practices that recognize that students learn differently and at a varied pace,

- classroom instruction that is designed, presented, and assessed in a manner that reflects student differences,

- teachers who use educational best practices, and are sensitive to the needs of diverse learners,

- the school ensuring quality educational settings for all students,

- the school obtaining sufficient funds, allocated in a fair and equitable manner,

- the school involving parents in an effective and collaborative manner,

- ongoing assessment of the program and feedback for needed improvement.

Inclusion: A Service, Not A Place, by Alan Gartner and Dorothy Kerzner Lipsky

QUALITY INDICATORS OF AN INCLUSIVE ENVIRONMENT

This scale can be used in a number of ways: as part of the planning process, as a school-assessment at a point in time, as a review of progress made or as a monitor of implementation.

SCHOOL CLIMATE	Not Yet Implemented	Partially Implemented	Fully Implemented
Responsibility for ("ownership") the education of all students is shared among the entire staff.			
There is collaboration between 1) evaluators and teachers, 2) general and special education teachers, and 3) classroom personnel and other service providers.			
Collaboration between and among staff is the instructional norm and is supported by administration and other arrangements (e.g. common "prep" periods, other arrangements for joint planning, collaborators have the opportunity to spend enough time together to become partners).			
The school's administrative organization, supervisory processes, and planning bodies reflect(s) and support(s) an inclusive environment (e.g. principal sees self as responsible for the learning of all students in the building, implementation of each student's IEP, supervision and evaluation of all personnel).			
Classrooms include students with disabilities in natural proportions.			
Self-contained classrooms, if present, are distributed throughout the building with classes of grade peers.			
Special education teachers, both those who teach in regular classes and those in self-contained classes, participate in all grade activities.			

COMPREHENSIVE EDUCATION PLAN	Not Yet Implemented	Partially Implemented	Fully Implemented
The school's planning documents and processes reflect(s) an inclusive environment (e.g. address issues of concern re: all students, including those with disabilities)			
The school leadership team reflects the full population of the school.			

CURRICULUM, INSTRUCTION & ASSESSMENT	Not Yet Implemented	Partially Implemented	Fully Implemented
Regular education program is strengthened so as to enable greater numbers of students to be served in that setting (i.e., good common school).			
Student needs are met while decreasing referrals and increasing decertification, thus providing increasing percentages of students with services in the general education environment, with needed supplementary aids and services.			
Classroom activities reflect the reality that students learn differently (in manner and rate).			
All staff working in general education classrooms are provided with all instructional materials for the regular curriculum.			
Students with disabilities are enabled to, and do, participate in the full range of the school's activities, including extra-curricular activities, with needed supplementary aids and services.			
Students with disabilities participate to the fullest extent appropriate in general education classes (N.B. This involves both assuring that such participation per the student's IEP is honored and a measure of overall "inclusion," viz. IDEA's presumption that students with disabilities will be educated with their nondisabled peers, with needed supplementary aids and services.)			
Students with disabilities are included in the state- and district-wide assessment, with needed adaptations and modifications, and their results are incorporated in the school's overall reporting.			

STAFF DEVELOPMENT	Not Yet Implemented	Partially Implemented	Fully Implemented
The school's professional development activities address the needs of all staff (including special educators) to serve all students (including those with disabilities), so as to assure beneficial access to the general curriculum.			

	Not Yet Implemented	Partially Implemented	Fully Implemented
SUPPORT SERVICES Support and clinical staff are effectively incorporated as integral members of the school community, in roles re: "prevention" and support services, as well as student assessment and as related services providers.			
PARENT INVOLVEMENT Parents of students with disabilities are included in all school activities (e.g., membership on the School Leadership Team and similar bodies, participation in the school's PA, involvement in other school activities).			
RESOURCES The building's resources are appropriately and equitably distributed so as to benefit all students. The resources are provided in a "placement neutral" manner, i.e. they follow the student and are not dependent on service setting.			
SCHOOL SELF-EVALUATION There is ongoing building self-evaluation to monitor progress toward goal of restructuring for quality education for all students.			

Inclusion: A Service, Not A Place, by Alan Gartner and Dorothy Kerzner Lipsky

3

Developing a Student's Program: The Work of the IEP Team

Just for the fun of it: Test your knowledge of the work of the IEP Team.

Who must be a part of the IEP Team? What are their differing roles?

_____

_____

Turn to page 37 to read about this topic.

What is the role of the regular education teacher in the development of a student's IEP?

_____

_____

Turn to page 38 to read about this topic.

What are the benefits of involving a regular education teacher in the development of student's IEP? For the student? For the teachers?

_____

_____

Turn to page 38 to read about this topic.

How can one assess the IEP?

_____

_____

Turn to page 39 to read about this topic.

What are the roles of the IEP Team members?

The IEP, according to the U.S. Department of Education *Final Regulations* on IDEA, is "the primary tool for enhancing the child's involvement and progress in the general curriculum."[9] In the development of the IEP, federal law requires a multi-disciplinary team; actual membership is determined by state law and regulation, so long as it falls within the broad requirements of IDEA. The following *must* be involved on the IEP Team: the child's parent(s) or guardian(s), a person who can interpret evaluation results, special education teacher(s) or provider(s), and a representative of the school district of the student's residence. In addition, *as appropriate*, for the individual student,[10] regular education teacher(s) at the child's grade level (see following section for details about this), others with knowledge or special expertise about the child, and transition service agency representative(s) are also included.

The child's parent brings both the most extensive knowledge of the student and the deepest commitment to her/his development. The student represents her/his own needs and documents the reality of the process by her/his presence. The presence of varied professionals reflects the multitude of vantage points that must be considered. A representative of the school district brings to the process information about the nature of services at the various schools in the district; this person must have the authority to commit resources and be able to ensure that whatever services are set out in the IEP will actually be provided. Whenever the purpose of the meeting is to discuss a child's transition needs or services, the school must invite a representative of any other agency likely to be providing and/or paying for such services.

Without specifying the particulars of the Team's functioning, it is to be governed by team decision making, which IDEA promotes as a process built upon consensus among the members. Should consensus not be reached, there are procedures (e.g., mediation, impartial hearing, access to the courts) available both to parents and to school personnel. While the law identifies the information which must be included in the IEP, it does not specify its form or appearance. Each state may decide what its IEP will look like; in several states, individual school districts design their own IEP.

The law requires that a program be designed to meet the student's needs, not that a student be shoe-horned into whatever program the district has available. Increasingly, there is the recognition that there are many program alternatives that can address a student's individual needs. Familiarity with these program options can enhance the quality of the IEP Team's deliberations. For parents, the opportunity to visit various program options can enhance the placement decision.

What is the role of the regular education teacher in the development of the student's IEP?

The reauthorized IDEA requires participation on the IEP Team of one or more regular education teachers at the child's grade level, if the child is or may be participating in the general education environment. The decision about such participation belongs to the IEP Team. Many districts now routinely include a regular education teacher at such meetings, rather than deny parents the right to participate in this decision.

The participation of a regular education teacher in that process brings to the table someone knowledgeable about that curriculum. At the same time, s/he can identify the supplementary aids and services needed both by the student and school staff. The federal regulations make clear the role of the regular education teacher as part of the IEP Team. "[T]he regular education teacher who is a member of the IEP Team must participate in discussions and decisions about how to modify the general curriculum in the regular classroom to ensure the child's involvement and progress in the general curriculum and participation in the regular education environment."[11]

What are the roles of related services providers?

Related services are not ends in themselves; rather, they are activities designed to enable students to benefit from the special education services. Increasingly schools are developing related services programs that are integrated into the overall special or general education program. As students with disabilities receive a greater portion of their services in the general education classroom, related services are provided on a "push-in" basis; that is, in the regular classroom. This serves four primary functions: it offers the services in a natural rather than separate setting; it is more likely to be integrated into the regular curriculum, it reduces the amount of time that the student is removed from the regular classroom, with the consequence of activities missed and the (negative) attention of moving in and out; and it provides an opportunity for general education students to receive the benefit of the services, e.g., speech, counseling, physical or occupational therapy, or specialized reading. More fundamental than the location of the service is that related services be integrated with the core curriculum.

The participation of related services providers at the IEP Team meeting is not required by law. Their participation, however, facilitates the integration of related services in the student's overall program. Related services providers must be given the completed IEP, and it is their responsibility to address the stated objectives.

How can the development of the IEP be enhanced?

When the development of the IEP is separate in time and location, rather than an integrated approach, those involved with its implementation may find themselves engaged in separate activities rather than one based on the curriculum. The participation of the regular education teacher as part of the IEP Team is a step toward reducing that separation. The participation of related services providers is also valuable. Opportunities for members of the IEP Team to observe the student in classroom activities offer an additional step toward integration. Ongoing team review of student progress is essential. These do not have to be formal IEP Team meetings. When decisions are made that materially change the IEP, the meeting must be formal.

Assessing the process and product of the IEP

The IEP process, both its development and implementation, is an ongoing one. As a Team and individually,[12] the following questions can serve as a guide in the IEP development and assessment.

The Content and Development Process of the IEP

Expected Outcomes

1. What are expected outcomes for children at this age/grade/educational level? Have the following been considered: academic outcomes, social/emotional outcomes, health/medical outcomes, life-skill outcomes, communication outcomes, vocational/career outcomes?

2. Are these appropriate outcomes for the student with a disability?

3. Should any of these outcomes be modified given the student's disability and its impact upon performance?

4. How should these (modified, if warranted) outcomes be reflected in the IEP goals and objectives?

5. How does the student's learning styles impact on IEP goals and objectives? In light of these, what modifications are needed in instructional methods? Curriculum? Learning environment? Instructional materials? How will these modifications be made? By whom?

6. What related and support services are necessary, in light of the goals and objectives?

7. What support and professional development needs are there for staff regarding curriculum modification? Consultation? Instructional strategies? In-class supports? Behavior?

8. How will needed planning time be provided? Who will be involved?

9. What has/has not worked in the past? In school? At home? In other settings?

Tools/Methods to Be Used to Measure Progress

1. Which of the following will be used to measure the student's academic performance: Teacher-developed testing? School/district/state standardized testing? Norm-referenced tests? Criterion-referenced tests? Review of homework/classwork? Task analyses? Mastery levels? Portfolio assessments? Performance? Parent input? Per IEP goals?

2. Which of the following will be used to measure the student's social/emotional development: Observation of on-task behavior? Observation of peer and adult/student interactions? Results of group and individual work? Self-reports? Parent reports? Per IEP goals?

3. Per these tools, is the student on track toward the established outcomes/goals? If not, are all the services being provided? Are they appropriate? Do they need to be modified/supplemented/changed? How does the student's performance compare with her/his classmates/age peers/district expectations?

Adapted from SPAN materials

Where can I find additional information about the work of the IEP Team?

In addition to the law and its Regulations (see previous chapter), the Office of Special Education and Rehabilitative Services (OSERS), U.S. Department of Education, has issued *A Guide to the Individualized Education Program*, July 2000.

See also,

Clark, S. G. (Nov/Dec 2000), "The IEP process as a tool for collaboration," *Teaching Exceptional Children*, 33(2), 56–66.

Creating a quality IEP. (January 1999). New York: New York City Board of Education.

IEP workbook: From evaluation through implementation. (1998). Chicago, IL: Chicago Public Schools.

Kukic, S. & Schrag, J. (1998). *IEP connections for a dynamic, living, and practical process: IEP Team member's manual.* (1998). Longmont, CO: Sopris West.

Student improvement is Job #1: Monitoring student progress. (February 1996). IO: Iowa Department of Education.

4

Collaboration

Just for the fun of it: Test yourself on your current knowledge of collaboration.

What are the benefits of collaborating with another teacher?

_____

_____

_____

Turn to page 44 to read about this topic.

What are the benefits of collaboration for students?

_____

_____

_____

Turn to page 45 to read about this topic.

What are the various models of collaboration?

_____

_____

_____

Turn to page 45 to read about this topic.

What are the advantages and disadvantages of the various models?

_____

_____

_____

Turn to page 48 to read about this topic.

How can collaboration be practiced in the classroom?

_____

_____

_____

Turn to page 51 to read about this topic.

What is collaboration?

Collaboration is the practice that allows *all* staff in the school to share responsibility for meeting the needs of *all* students. There are a great variety of ways in which collaboration can take place. For the participants, collaboration involves a process of change from the traditional solo practice of an individual teacher and her/his class to partners working together to address the needs of all the students in the classroom. The partners share their knowledge, step out of their old roles ("role release"); and each learns from and is dependent upon the other (interdependency). Teachers have identified that the "doing of collaboration" becomes a powerful means of professional and personal development. While some teachers may initially be reluctant to collaborate with another staff member across the country, the idea is gaining widespread acceptance.

What are the benefits of collaboration for teachers and students?

The increasing body of knowledge that students are expected to master, as well as the increasing diversity of America's classrooms, requires a pedagogic shift. The past model was based on one teacher providing all the needed instruction to all the students in her/his classroom; the new model is based on an education service delivery model in which two or more professionals work collaboratively to teach the material to a diverse group of learners. For the increasing number of students with disabilities served in general education classes, as well as for other students with special needs that are not identified, the collaboration of teachers with different styles, approaches, knowledge and skills allows for the teaching of the general education curricula with enhanced outcomes for all students.

The concept of teacher collaboration is in sharp contrast with the traditional *consultative model*, where one teacher (the consultant) is seen as more knowledgeable and the other (the consultee) is seen as in need of that expertise. In the collaborative model, two (or more) teachers have different expertise and each is expected to contribute toward the shared enterprise of providing educational opportunities for all the students.

From the perspective of the teachers, there are many benefits of collaboration. These include:

- reducing the isolation of being a solitary teacher,
- enjoying the collaboration with a colleague,
- sharing the responsibility for the teaching of a diverse group of students,
- learning new skills and approaches, and
- having a non-supervisory colleague reflect on your practice.

A range of benefits for students have been identified as a result of collaborative teaching. These include students:

- having a wider range of instructional alternatives,
- receiving less fragmented instruction (especially students with special needs),
- being less critical of others and more motivated,
- recognizing abilities among peers,
- improving academic performance,
- improving social skills,
- relating to several adults,
- developing positive peer relationships,
- seeing adults work together cooperatively,
- seeing adults disagree and work through difference(s), and
- increasing their sense of community.

"The self-contained [special education] program assumes a ceiling on what the kids can do. With the support of two teachers in the mainstream classroom, there's no ceiling." A high school special education teacher, cited in "After initial reluctance, co-teachers say they wouldn't have it any other way," (March/April, 1999) *Harvard Education Letter*, 15(2), p. 3.

"Before we started co-teaching, I basically didn't know what my children were doing outside my room; they just went somewhere and did something. They would miss whatever was going on in my class. I wouldn't schedule a test at that time, but they missed the lesson that hour or sometimes they even missed story time, the fun part. They had to miss something. Now [with co-teaching], I'm able to expand on what they have learned." An elementary general education teacher, cited in J. E. Nowacek (1992), Professionals talk about teaching together: Interviews with five collaborating teachers, *Intervention in school and clinic*, 27, p. 263.]

The benefits of collaboration have been affirmed by many teachers and few choose to go back to solo practice. The culture of schools, however, often is one of isolation, where success is measured more individually than as a result of the whole team's effort. Teachers are too often cloistered behind the classroom door, and contact with colleagues, as one teacher put it, is "brief, incomplete and often inconsequential."[13] If collaboration is to succeed, it must be intentional, structured, and supported.

Professional development and opportunities to plan together are key to effective collaboration. Frequently, teacher education programs have prepared general and special education teachers in separate and isolated pre-service programs. They have provided few opportunities for future teachers to learn how to work together with a more diverse student population in restructured inclusive education classrooms. While changes are necessary at the pre-service level, professional development opportunities must be a central aspect of a school district's efforts. This includes training in joint planning, collaboration, co-teaching, curricular adaptation, enhanced instructional strategies, classroom management, and assessment. The focus of the professional development should be on situation-specific problem-solving; it should address the change process itself.

Professional development for restructured and inclusive education involves a paradigmatic shift from traditional in-service and teacher training models. In the traditional model, the teacher, either general or special education, was a qualified professional who taught in her/his own classroom. Upgrading and/or expansion of the teacher's skills was based upon the teacher's particular interest(s). In the new inclusive classroom, special and general educators come to rely upon each other's skills and knowledge, and to develop ways to work collaboratively as a team. During professional development, inclusion brings together teachers as peers, each as a "trainee" and "trainer," collaborating to become quality teachers of all students.

The process of professional development models the collaboration of the inclusive classroom, and the relationship between the two teachers models for the students adults working together. Indeed, one of the frequent reports from successful collaborating teachers is that the students see them working together, including resolving differences in a peaceful manner.

Collaboration differs from the traditional model of the solo teacher in her/his classroom; what the late Al Shanker, past president of the American Federation of Teachers, used to call the "egg crate classroom." The collaborative model means that the services the student needs are provided by the collaborating teachers. Both are the child's teacher. As such, parents should come to know both and share with both their dreams for the child and their sense of the classroom experience.

What are the models of collaboration?

There is not one approach to collaboration. Schools often use more than one model to address the needs of their students and teachers. Among the various models in use, the six that follow are the most frequently cited:

1. *Co-teaching, full-time:* the most typical model. A special and general education teacher are in the same classroom, jointly sharing full responsibility for the entire class.

2. *Co-teaching, part-time:* a variation of the above. A special education teacher divides her/his time between two general education classrooms. When the special education teacher is in the classroom,

the teachers will address the major academic subjects. In some districts, a paraprofessional is assigned to the class when the special education teacher is in the other class.

3. *Indirect support:* the special education teacher provides consultative or "indirect" support to the regular education teacher in whose class students with disabilities are included.

4. *Methods and resources:* a special education teacher has primary responsibility for adapting materials and developing alternative instructional strategies for a number of students, often in different classrooms.

5. *Team model:* a special education teacher is incorporated as part of the team of general education teachers, which then serves a cohort of students, general and special education. This is a common middle school design.[14] It provides an opportunity for all of the teachers who serve students who move from class-to-class to share information about the students and the course work. At the elementary level, a special education teacher may be assigned to a grade level or work in a specific content area.

6. *School-wide model:* the entire staff as a group take on responsibility for all students, disabled and nondisabled, teaching in a multitude of configurations, e.g., lecturing to a large group, tutoring a small group, etc.

Suggestions for Teachers: Co-teaching Approaches

Co-teaching is the most common of the collaboration approaches. Based on their individual strengths and interests, teachers have developed many arrangements for teaching together. It is the mixture and flexibility of these arrangements that makes the collaborative process a positive experience for both teachers. The common features are that the teachers plan together, alternate roles, and students are not divided, special and general education.

The following collaboration arrangements have been identified by teachers:

- *Team teaching:* both teachers deliver the same instruction at the same time.
- *Alternative teaching:* one teacher takes responsibility for a large group while the other works with a smaller group;
- *Station teaching:* teachers divide both content and students, and switch and repeat;
- *Parallel teaching:* both teachers are presenting the same material simultaneously, dividing the class into two groups;
- *One teach, one rotate through the classroom:* one teacher has primary responsibility for the delivery of the material, while the other circulates through the room providing assistance to the students as needed; and

- *One teach, one observe:* one teacher presents the material while the other observes the lesson and student reaction, and subsequently shares observations with his/her colleague.

Advantages and disadvantages of the various co-teaching approaches?

The collaborative models and approaches identified in the previous section each have advantages and disadvantages. They have been identified as follows (Friend, 2001).

Method	Advantages	Disadvantages
Team teaching	• Lower student-teacher ratio • Highest level of teacher collaboration	• Most complex • Most dependent upon teachers' styles of teaching
Alternative teaching	• Smaller group size • Students remain part of the community • Can use to provide enrichment, as well as support	• Can become a segregated program
Parallel teaching	• Small groups • Better student participation • Strategic grouping of students • More effective discipline	• Higher noise level • Students more easily distracted • Both teachers need to know the content • Need to cover content in similar ways • High level of trust needed between the teachers
One teach, one rotate	• Assistance regularly provided to students as needed	• One teacher put in the role of an assistant; is this the best use of professional expertise?
One teach, one observe	• More detailed observation of student learning. • Effective planning together, based on observations of student learning.	• One teacher put in the role of an assistant; is this the best use of professional expertise?

Gately and Gately (2001) emphasize interpersonal communications as key to co-teaching, identifying three stages based upon the nature of the communication.[15]

- Beginning stage: Guarded, careful communication

- Compromising stage: Give and take communication, with a sense of having to "give" to "get"

- Collaborating stage: Open communication and interaction, mutual admiration.[16]

They point out that at the beginning stage teachers seek to establish a professional working relationship, developing a sense of boundaries and permeabilities. For some general education teachers, there may be a sense of intrusion and invasion, while for some special education teachers there may be a sense of discomfort and exclusion. Teachers tread slowly and cautiously. Unless there is recognition of a developmental process, teachers may get "stuck" at this stage.

The compromising stage is one of give and take, with the compromises made (e.g., giving up something in order to gain something else) becoming the basis for a more collaborative process.

In the collaborative stage, there is more open communication, and a greater degree of comfort and use of humor. This is experienced not only by the teachers, but the students as well. The two teachers work together and complement each other. It has been said that students in an inclusive classroom sometimes find it difficult to discern which teacher is the special educator and which the general educator; both are teachers, no adjectives!

How does collaboration fit into IDEA?

Collaboration is a way to address the law's presumption that students with disabilities will be served in a general education setting, with the needed supports. The law emphasizes "whole school" approaches for the education of students with disabilities. Collaboration is one of the ways that such an approach can become a reality.

The following imaginary conversation highlights the shift from separate special education services to a collaborative approach:

- "I do it all by myself," says the special education teacher of a self-contained class.
- "I do the special part myself," says the resource or "pull out" teacher or related services provider.
- "Someone else does it," says the general education teacher.
- "We do it together," says the collaboration of regular and special educators.

  [Adapted from DeBoer & Fister, 1994, p. 11]

While collaboration is most often considered a matter between classroom teachers, additional forms of collaboration are worth noting. These include collaboration between classroom personnel and the providers of related and resource room services. When IEP services for a student are conducted on a "pull out" basis, often they divert attention from the general education curriculum, disrupt the classroom as children move in and out, and cause students pulled out to miss important learning opportunities in the general education classroom. Increasingly, related and resource room services are being provided on a "push in"[17] basis, with these specialists infusing their services within the context of the general education curriculum and classroom.[18] A further advantage of this "push in" design is that other students, those "at risk" but not labeled as "disabled," or other general education students all can benefit from such in-class services.

Another aspect of collaboration is between those involved in student evaluation, program design and classroom personnel. The evaluation and IEP development process too often has been separate from the classroom activities of the student. The reauthorized IDEA requirement for the participation of a general education teacher, at the child's grade level, as a member of the IEP Team, is intended to enhance the integration of the IEP development and the classroom implementation. Additionally, opportunities for other members of the IEP Team to observe students in the classroom and to offer services within the classroom are further areas for collaboration.

Paraprofessionals have become an integral part of inclusion. This term encompasses those staff members with such titles as teacher aide, teacher assistant, and paraeducator. When teachers have the support of a paraprofessional, collaboration is essential. Early in the implementation of P.L. 94–142, most paraprofessionals were assigned to provide assistance to individual students. In recent years, the focus has shifted for paraprofessionals to work in the classroom under the guidance of the general education teacher rather than with an individual student. It is important that s/he not be "velcroed" to the child with a disability, which could inhibit the student's interaction with other students in the classroom and create a dependency that is not in the best interest of the child.

To be an effective member of the classroom's instructional team, paraprofessionals require professional development. This could include a balance between professional development exclusively with other paraprofessionals and professional development with teachers. An additional feature for paraprofessionals is the opportunity in a growing number of school districts for them to participate in a career ladder program, earning a college degree and becoming certified as a teacher. In many communities, the implementation of career ladder programs has led to positive developments: an increase in the number of teachers from the same communities as the students, teachers with a greater likelihood of staying in the school system, and teachers who begin their work as professionals with a great deal of prior experience in the schools.

The components of classroom collaboration include:

- *Sharing responsibility:* A change from the sense of ownership of "my" classroom to a shared responsibility, in planning and delivery; also, taking responsibility for all students,

- *Developing a shared classroom approach:* Each will need to work with the other professional in developing classroom practices, rules, and activities,

- *Learning collaborative skills:* Each will need to learn the pedagogic and personal skills of collaboration, including who implements what curricula material, in which manner, for which students, and how to express disagreement,

- *Learning from each other:* Each must learn the assumptions, perspectives, knowledge language and jargon used by the partner, particularly as it relates to the other's training and expertise; and her/his field, and

- *Exposure:* Each must learn to accept the close observation of her/his practice by another adult. This involves a level of exposure of one's practice that is new for most teachers and may be difficult for some. Collaborative teams, over time, express their sense of relief that they no longer are expected to know everything and appreciate the sense of comradery.

What are the stages of collaboration?

In the process of implementing collaboration, four stages can be considered.

STAGE 1:

Establishing the context: Basic to collaboration is the acceptance of shared responsibility and a commitment toward all the students in the classroom. Some teachers have called this shared "ownership," or an inclusive "community of learners." There is a recognition at this stage that collaboration cannot be done without planning and discussion, sometimes including differences and disagreements.

The metaphor of a dance has been used to describe co-teaching and the process of collaboration that underlies it. "Like all dances, we must first hear the music, then learn the steps, maintain our balance, and coordinate with our partner. The actual 'messiness' of our collaborative interactions probably compares more to the 1960s rock and roll than to a stylized ballet, but the synchrony is there, nevertheless." (Halvorsen & Neary, 2001, p. 130).

STAGE 2:

Negotiating the basis of the relationship: When two teachers plan to work together in the classroom, regardless of the particular model, there are a number of questions that they should ask each other. These are called "points of negotiation" and addressing them can become the basis upon which to forge an effective partnership. There are no "right" answers to these points of negotiation. Done prior to the beginning of collaboration, they become the basis for the partners to work together. And, over time they should be revisited.

"There were times when we disagreed, and we learned to compromise and sometimes to give the final decision to the other teacher. Our classroom management styles were also different, but we learned to find a compromise that worked for both of us. Most important, I think it was critical to inform our students of what we were doing and why. Our students understood that they would have two teachers, with equal authority and with whom they would have equal opportunities to work. Many of my students expressed that having two teachers is better because everyone gets more help." A classroom teacher in N. L. Langerock (Nov/Dec 2000), "A passion for action research," *Teaching Exceptional Children*, 33(2), p. 27.

Overall, in developing the partnership the participants should consider the following points:

- The partnership is a professional relationship, requiring respect and acceptance of shared responsibility. The metaphor of a marriage is not appropriate.

- View the collaboration as an evolving relationship, not an instant arrangement.

- Structure the roles to ensure responsibility for all students is shared between both participants. From the students' point of view, this means they each have two teachers.

- Utilize teaching strategies that take advantage of the strengths of each of the participants.

- Evaluate the collaborative process on an ongoing basis, as well as in terms of student outcomes.

The Blackline Master No. 9, pg. 56, "Points of Negotiation in Collaborative Teaching," can serve as a basis for discussion between the collaborators.

STAGE 3:

Planning together: No factor is more important to the success of this effort than opportunity for the partners to have regularly scheduled planning time. When teachers plan together, the following should support that effort:

- regularly scheduled sessions that have a fixed start and end time,

- planned agendas,

- prior preparation and active participation of each team member,
- interruptions should be held to an absolute minimum,
- administrators should not assign teachers for another duty during planning time.

As the school's leader, the principal plays an essential role in ensuring that time for staff planning is scheduled. Schools have developed a variety of ways of accomplishing planning time. Among them are:

- common "prep" periods for the collaborating teachers,
- a "floating" substitute teacher to release the collaborating teachers,
- "per session" time, before or after school,
- compensatory time,
- as part of an assigned professional activity,
- release from other duty,
- staff development days/afternoons,
- class coverage by other staff,
- incorporation within an extended instructional day,
- as part of a restructured school week/year,
- administrators, deans, counselors covering a class,
- students engaged in an activity with another adult, and
- dropping less essential activities.

STAGE 4:

Assessing the outcomes of collaboration: There are two sets of outcomes that warrant attention: outcomes for students, based on the standards of the curriculum, and outcomes involved in the collaboration process itself. In assessing outcomes for students, it is the school's and district's regular measures and practices that should be used, e.g., standardized tests, portfolios and performances, classroom participation, etc. The Blackline Master No. 10, pg. 57–58, "Assessing Collaboration: A Team Study Guide," may be used as a guide to assess the process of collaboration.

The Co-teaching Rating Scale (CRS) is another design to examine the effectiveness of co-teaching classrooms.[19] It can be used by teachers who co-teach full- or part-time. It can enable the teachers to identify areas of their collaboration that are successful, as well as to focus on areas that may need improvement. It can serve as a tool in developing co-teaching goals. There are two scales, one for the special education teacher and the other for the general education teacher. Each form asks similar questions. It is best for the teachers to complete the form independently and then to compare and discuss their answers. (See pages 59–60.)

What are the roles of other school personnel regarding collaboration?

To be successful, collaboration must be an essential aspect of the entire school program. Schoolwide collaboration means that all the personnel of the building work together to address the needs of all students, not only a few teachers. Administrators must convey the message attitudinal and organizationally.

Collaboration involves a mind-set—one that recognizes that *all* students belong and *all* staff are responsible for the success of each and every student. The organization and procedures of the school are designed to express an inclusive environment; this involves a shift from a focus on "my" students to "our" students.

The necessary restructuring can take place only when collaboration is implemented as a schoolwide approach. In this, the school's administration plays an essential role. This includes the following:

- teacher schedules and student programs are developed to reflect the collaboration.

- the supervision and evaluation of collaborating teachers incorporates the realities of the collaboration. Thus, for example, if the model of collaboration used, for a particular subject, involves one of the partners presenting the material and the other reinforcing it, the evaluation of each should take this into account.

- time is provided for the partners to plan and work together, not as a frill but as an essential part of the school's procedures.

- support and consultative services are available to the collaborators.

- a "universal design" approach is encouraged, rather than a single instructional approach that has to be modified for individual students.

- the school recognizes diversity among students, not on a demographic basis but as expressed as differences in learning "styles," or "intelligences," or level of knowledge and skill in a particular subject area, or pace of learning.

Where can I find additional information regarding collaboration?

Bauwens, J. & Mueller, P. H. (2000). Maximizing the mindware of human resources. In R. A. Villa & J. S. Thousand (Eds.), *Restructuring for caring and effective education: Piecing the puzzle together*, (pp. 328–359). Baltimore, MD: Paul H. Brookes Publishing Co.

DeBoer, A. & Fister, S. (1995). *Working together: Tools for collaborative teaching*. Longmont, CO: Sopris West.

Dieker, L. (2000). *Co-teaching lesson plan book*. Reston, VA: Council for Exceptional Children.

Friend, M. (2001), *Successful co-teaching: Improving the success of your inclusive program.* Bellevue, WA: Bureau of Education and Research.

Friend, M. & Cook, L. (1996). *Interactions: Collaboration skills for school professionals.* White Plains, NY: Longman.

Giangreco, M. F., Prelock, P. A., Reid, R. R., Dennis, R. E., & Edelman, S. W. (2000). Roles of related services personnel in inclusive schools. In R. A. Villa & J. S. Thousand (Eds)., *Restructuring for caring and effective schools: Piecing the puzzle together,* (pp. 360–388). Baltimore, MD: Paul H. Brookes Publishing Co.

Halvorsen, A. T. & Neary, T. (2001). *Building inclusive schools: Tools and strategies for success.* Boston, MA: Allyn & Bacon.

McGregor, G. & Vogelsberg, R. T. (1999). *Inclusive schooling practices: Pedagogical and research findings: A synthesis of the literature that informs best practices about inclusive education.* Baltimore, MD: Paul H. Brookes Publishing Co.

Snell, M. E. & Janney, R. (2000). *Teachers' guides to inclusive practices: Collaborative Teaming.* Baltimore, MD: Paul H. Brookes Publishing Co.

Vaughn, S., Schumm, J. S. & Arguelles, M. E. (Nov/Dec 1997), "The ABCDEs of co-teaching," *Teaching Exceptional Children,* pp. 4–10.

POINTS OF NEGOTIATION IN COLLABORATIVE TEACHING:
A SELF-STUDY GUIDE

It is important for teams to discuss their differences and similarities. The items below have been identified as important by teachers. Complete this survey individually, and then discuss your responses with your collaborator.

Instructional methods:

What instructional methods do I currently use?
What additional ones would I like to use?

Instructional materials:

What instructional materials do I currently use?
What additional ones would I like to use?

Assignments:

How do I currently handle student assignments? In class? As homework? What are alternative ways of handling them? With which would I be most uncomfortable?

Testing and assessment:

How do I currently handle testing and assessment? What alternative ways are there? With which alternative methods would I be most uncomfortable?

Class rules:

What are my current class rules? What alternative rules might be established? What rules would be most uncomfortable for me?

Communication:

How do I like to communicate with a colleague? What ways are preferred? What ways would be most uncomfortable for me?

Division of work:

What activities do I prefer to do? Not like to do? Would I prefer rotation of roles or a fixed division of assignments between us?

Problem solving:

How do I handle disagreements with another adult? What is most comfortable for me? What is likely to bother me the most?

Planning:

How do I currently plan? How would I like to plan with a colleague? When would the best time be for me? Before school? After school? During school? No set time is necessary; we can do it on the "fly."

Inclusion: A Service, Not A Place, by Alan Gartner and Dorothy Kerzner Lipsky.

ASSESSING COLLABORATION: A TEAM STUDY GUIDE

It is important that partners periodically assess their collaboration. It is best to do this on an ongoing basis. After considering these issues individually, compare and discuss them with your collaborator and address any changes that should be made to strengthen your work together.

Planning:
Do we plan together? What are some examples of our planning, short- and long-range? How can we plan together better?

_____

_____

_____

_____

Interdependence:
Are we interdependent? What are some examples of our interdependence? What can we do to enhance our interdependence?

_____

_____

_____

_____

Learning from each other:
Do we learn from each other? What are some examples of our learning? How can we enhance such learning?

_____

_____

_____

_____

Satisfaction:
Am I satisfied with our work? Our collaboration? What can I do to enhance our collaboration? What can I ask my partner to do?

_____

_____

_____

_____

(continued on next page)

Contributions:
Are each of our contributions of equal value? To the extent they are not,
what can each of us do?

_____

_____

_____

_____

Communication:
How well do we communicate? How well do we handle disagreements?
How might we do this better? What can I do? What can I ask my partner to do?

_____

_____

_____

_____

Reflection and evaluation of practice:
Do we reflect upon and evaluate our practice? How might we do this more/better?
How do we use such reflection and evaluation to improve our practice?
What might we do more/better?

_____

_____

_____

_____

Support:
Do we get the support from each other that we both/each need? If not,
what do I/we need? How might I/we go about getting this?

_____

_____

_____

_____

Parent involvement:
How well do parents know both of us? How can we work together as a team
to achieve greater parent involvement?

_____

_____

_____

_____

Inclusion: A Service, Not A Place, by Alan Gartner and Dorothy Kerzner Lipsky.

CO-TEACHING RATING SCALE: SPECIAL EDUCATION TEACHER FORMAT

Respond to each question below by circling the number that best describes your viewpoint.

1. Rarely   2. Sometimes   3. Usually

1. I can easily read the nonverbal cues of my coteaching partner.	1 2 3	
2. I feel comfortable moving freely about the space in the cotaught classroom.	1 2 3	
3. I understand the curriculum standards with respect to the content area in the cotaught classroom.	1 2 3	
4. Both teachers in the cotaught classroom agree on the goals of the cotaught classroom.	1 2 3	
5. Planning can be spontaneous, with changes occurring during the instructional lesson.	1 2 3	
6. I often present lessons in the cotaught classroom.	1 2 3	
7. Classroom rules & procedures have been jointly developed.	1 2 3	
8. Many measures are used for grading students.	1 2 3	
9. Humor is often used in the classroom.	1 2 3	
10. All materials are shared in the classroom.	1 2 3	
11. I am familiar with the methods & materials with respect to content areas.	1 2 3	
12. Modifications of goals for students with special needs are incorporated into this class.	1 2 3	
13. Planning for classes is the shared responsibility of both teachers.	1 2 3	
14. The "chalk" passes freely between the two teachers.	1 2 3	
15. A variety of classroom management techniques is used to enhance the learning of all students.	1 2 3	
16. Test modifications are commonplace.	1 2 3	
17. Communication is open and honest.	1 2 3	
18. There is fluid positioning of teachers in the classroom.	1 2 3	
19. I feel confident in my knowledge of the curriculum content.	1 2 3	
20. Student-centered objectives are incorporated into the curriculum.	1 2 3	
21. Time is allotted/found for common planning.	1 2 3	
22. Students accept both teachers as equal partners in the learning process.	1 2 3	
23. Behavior management is the shared responsibility of both teachers.	1 2 3	
24. Goals & objectives in IEPs are considered as part of the grading for students with special needs.	1 2 3	

From Gately and Gately

CO-TEACHING RATING SCALE: GENERAL EDUCATION TEACHER FORMAT

Respond to each question below by circling the number that best describes your viewpoint.

1. Rarely   2. Sometimes   3. Usually

1. I can easily read the nonverbal cues of my coteaching partner.   1 2 3

2. Both teachers move freely about the space in the cotaught classroom.   1 2 3

3. My coteacher understands the curriculum standards with respect to the content area in the cotaught classroom.   1 2 3

4. Both teachers in the cotaught classroom agree on the goals of the cotaught classroom.   1 2 3

5. Planning can be spontaneous with changes occurring during the instructional lesson.   1 2 3

6. My coteaching partner often presents lessons in the cotaught class   1 2 3

7. Classroom rules & routines have been jointly developed.   1 2 3

8. Many measures are used for grading students.   1 2 3

9. Humor is often used in the classroom.   1 2 3

10. All materials are shared in the classroom.   1 2 3

11. The special educator is familiar with the methods & materials with respect to the content area.   1 2 3

12. Modifications of goals for students with special needs are fully incorporated into this class.   1 2 3

13. Planning for classes is the shared responsibility of both teachers.   1 2 3

14. The "chalk" passes freely between the two teachers.   1 2 3

15. A variety of classroom management techniques is used to enhance the learning of all students.   1 2 3

16. Test modifications are commonplace.   1 2 3

17. Communication is open and honest.   1 2 3

18. There is fluid positioning of teachers in the classroom.   1 2 3

19. I am confident of the special educator's knowledge of the curriculum content.   1 2 3

20. Student-centered objectives are incorporated into the curriculum.   1 2 3

21. Time is allotted/found for common planning.   1 2 3

22. Students accept both teachers as equal partners in the learning process.   1 2 3

23. Behavior management is the shared responsibility of both teachers.   1 2 3

24. Goals & objectives in IEPs are considered as part of the grading of students with special needs.   1 2 3

From Gately and Gately

5

Supplementary Aids and Services in a Differentiated Classroom

Just for the fun of it: Test yourself on your current knowledge of supplementary aids and services, accommodations and modifications for differentiated classrooms.

What are supplementary aids and services in instruction?

_____

_____

Turn to page 62 to read about this topic.

What are accommodations and modifications in assessment?

_____

_____

Turn to page 62 to read about this topic

What is a differentiated classroom?

_____

_____

Turn to page 64 to read about this topic.

What are the differences/relationships among supplementary aids and services, accommodations and modifications, and a differentiated classroom?

_____

_____

Turn to page 65 to read about this topic

What criteria should be used in considering the appropriate supplementary aids and services for a student?

_____

_____

Turn to page 68 to read about this topic.

What are supplementary aids and services? Accommodations and modifications?

Supplementary aids and services are related to instructional activities. Accommodations and modifications are related to the students' demonstration of learning outcomes. Supplemental aids and services are designed to provide supports to students with disabilities to enable them to benefit from the educational services provided. Accommodations and modifications are designed to enable these students to demonstrate their learning. Supplementary aids and services are to instructional activities what accommodations and modifications are to assessment.

Supplementary aids and services are those services that a student or school, staff on the student's behalf, need to benefit from the school's offerings. As such, they can be as simple or as complex. They can relate to the *content* of the instruction (the curriculum), the *process* of presenting the curriculum (instructional strategies), the *setting* in which learning takes place (the environment). As part of the process of the development of the IEP, the Team must, for each student in each subject area, identify whether it is appropriate for the student to participate in the state- and district-wide assessment, and, if so, whether some or all accommodations and/or modifications are appropriate. While the federal law applies only to state- and district-wide assessment, good practice warrants the use of the same adaptations in classroom and school assessment activities.

When the learning consequence of the student's disability requires that a supplementary aid or service be provided for instruction, it is likely that a parallel accommodation or modification will be required in assessing the student's learning. For example, a student who requires instruction using Braille material will in all likelihood require Braille material for assessment. A student who needs extra time or material on tape or read to her/him to master the curriculum will in all likelihood require extra time or material on tape or read to her/him to demonstrate her/his knowledge on the assessment.

In the 1997 IDEA amendments, the Congress expressed the expectation that the great bulk of students with disabilities would participate in these assessments. When this is not to be the case, the IEP Team must describe how the student's learning will be assessed, i.e., an alternate assessment. The differences between accommodations, modifications, and alternate assessment are discussed on the pages that follow.

Historically, as students with disabilities have come to be served in general education classrooms, teachers have "retrofitted" the curriculum and adapted their instructional practices. Such adaptations would be specified on a student's IEP. Rather than a focus on the adaptations solely to address the needs of a student with a disability, a proactive approach has developed, designed to make the curriculum accessible to a diverse group of students.

> The task becomes one of integrating knowledge about curriculum and new curriculum trends with expectations about how learners with diverse characteristics will interact with the content. Through such collaborative discussions—and, then, actions—teachers can shape what goes on in the classroom to the advantage of all students before presenting content, rather than after a student encounters difficulty.[20]

The term "universal design" has been used to describe this "front-loading" or proactive approach. As a result, there is likely to be less need to provide specific adaptations for a student in a differentiated classroom, as that classroom has flexibility built in.

How do supplementary aids and services, and accommodations and modifications, relate to the law?

Providing individualized assistance to students has long been a hall-mark of special education programs, addressed since 1975 in the regulations derived from the federal law. In the 1997 reauthorized IDEA, the Congress increased the salience of supplementary aids and services by including them in the law itself. As part of each student's IEP, the IEP Team now must consider the needed supplementary aids and services, as well as needed accommodations and modifications in state- and district-wide assessments.

The provision of needed supplementary aids and services to students with disabilities served in general education classes marks the difference between "dumping" and the provision of the student's entitlement to an appropriate education in the least restrictive environment. The key to the development of appropriate supplementary aids and services to students with disabilities served in the general education environment are the provisions of the reauthorized IDEA. These include:

- regular education teachers, at the student's grade level, are to be a part of the team that develops each student's IEP, if the child is, or may be, participating in general education classes.

- the regular education teacher, as a member of the IEP Team, is to participate in the development of the IEP, including determination of needed program modifications, supplementary aids and services as support for the student and school personnel. The general education teacher must also participate in the review and revision of the IEP and ensure the necessary supports for the student *and* the teacher so as to enable the child to succeed in the general education classroom.

- enhanced federal support for professional development, including that of general education personnel who serve students with disabilities.

In developing the IEP, the Team must consider the student's strengths, parental concerns, and the results of the most recent evaluation. To address the unique needs of each student, the IEP Team must consider:

- behavioral interventions, i.e., strategies including positive behavioral interventions and supports to address behaviors that impede learning;[21]

- language needs, i.e., in the case of a student who is limited English proficient, the IEP Team must consider the language needs of the student;

- communication needs, i.e., in the case of a student who is deaf or hard of hearing, the IEP Team must consider the language and communication needs of the student;

- instruction in Braille, i.e., in the case of a child who is blind or visually impaired, the prescribed program must provide instruction in Braille and the use of Braille, unless the IEP Team determines that instruction in Braille or the use of Braille is not appropriate; and

- assistive technology devices and services.[22]

What are differentiated classrooms and "best practices" for them?

A differentiated classroom can serve all the students in a school. The focal point of the classroom is the students, not the curriculum. It builds on the premise that students are different in their readiness, interests, and needs in each curriculum area. In the differentiated classroom, the teacher varies the material, the instructional approach, and the manner in which the students demonstrate their learning.

The Differentiated Classroom

A differentiated classroom incorporates many of current educational reform ideas. These include:

- students and teachers work to be respectful of each other by accepting and appreciating one another's similarities and differences,

- teachers continually gather information about students' current readiness, interests, and learning style(s),

- teachers use information gathered about students to provide varied learning options and to build learning around important concepts,

- all students take part in learning experiences that are interesting, important, and powerful,

- students use essential skills to complete open-ended problems designed to help them make sense of key concepts and principles,

- teachers present lessons at several different levels to ensure appropriate challenge for students at varied readiness levels,
- teachers offer students learning choices centered around topics of study, ways of learning, avenues of expression, and working conditions,
- information is presented to students in varied ways, including orally, visually, demonstration, part to whole, and whole to part; varied instructional approaches are used to address individual student needs,
- students collaborate with other students and teachers,
- teachers serve as "coaches" who attend to individual students as well as to the whole class; teachers move each student along a continuum of growth; learning has no ceiling,
- groups are developed in classrooms according to need, but they are varied to ensure against tracking,
- teachers design homework to extend individual student's understanding,
- varied assessment options are provided,
- grades or reports to parents are based largely on individual growth.[23]

Many of the concepts of a differentiated classroom have proven effective in earlier educational innovations, e.g., the Adaptive Learning Environment Model (ALEM), developed in the 1980's by Margaret Wang. A differentiated classroom is supported by Gardner's formulation that students have "multiple intelligences," and that among them they have "jagged profiles." That is, a student may have strengths in some areas of the intelligences, and less in other ones. (See pages 78 and 79.)

A number of factors have been identified in a differentiated or student-focused classroom. In particular, the teacher makes an ongoing effort at differentiating *what* is taught, *how* the teaching approach responds to student differences, and *why* particular materials are used or modified to enhance learning. The basic features of a differentiated classroom include variations in instructional strategies, organizational strategies, and environmental supports.

Instructional strategies that support a differentiated classroom:
- Stations: different locations in the classroom where groups or individual students can work on various tasks simultaneously and then progress to another station,
- Centers: physical locations in the classroom for distinct topical areas (e.g., science, art, writing, etc.),
- Cooperative learning: students work in small groups with members at different levels of expertise,[24]

- Multiple intelligences: offers varying entry points into a subject (e.g., narration, logical/quantitative, aesthetic, musical, experiential, environmental), as well as ways to pursue content and demonstrate outcomes,

- Multi-level instruction: maintains a common focus on essential learning/skills, while enabling a tiering of experiences and outcomes: the teacher identifies the learning expected of all students, of most students, and of a few students, and addresses all three groups in the lesson,

- Learning contracts: A student works independently, while maintaining teacher direction of what is to be learned, and

- Universal design: A variety of formats is used in presenting curricula, in terms of physical access to the material (e.g., text, speech, large print, Braille, graphically), learning access (e.g., material at various reading levels[25]), and cognitive access (e.g., embedding prompts and questions in the text that encourage reciprocal teaching).

Organizational strategies that support a differentiated classroom:

Directions:

- start the class with a familiar activity, and then meet with small groups as to their specific activity,

- alert the group to tomorrow's tasks; use task cards that identify the task at a work station or center,

- tape-record instructions; put directions on a flip chart or chalkboard.

Student-teacher signaling systems:

- students use a sign or flagging system on their desk to let the teacher know they have completed the work or need help,

- students write their names on the chalkboard,

- student taking a number,

- teacher classroom signals to control noise levels.

Organization:

- establish positive behavior rules and consequences for positive or negative behavior,

- student work folders and organized/coded places for student work,

- listing skills and competencies for various activities,

- expand the skills and competencies to lesser and more advanced levels,

- take notes as you rotate around the classroom,

- establish start-up and closing procedures for activities.

Physical environment supports of a differentiated classroom:

- Floor space: allows for students with physical mobility needs,

- Furniture arrangement: encourages students working together;

- Equipment and computers: availability for all students, with adequate storage space for student work.

What are supplementary aids and services "best practices"?

Supplementary aids and services are the instructional supports needed by students and their teacher(s) to enable the student to succeed in the general education environment. These can include:

- adaptations in the physical environment,

- adaptations in tasks assigned and materials provided,

- curricular adaptations and modifications,

- alternative instructional strategies,

- use of additional personnel (e.g., paraprofessionals and classroom aides),

- consultation between the classroom teacher(s) and other school/agency personnel,[26]

- behavior intervention plans,

- use of assistive technology.

Supplementary aids and services can be organized in multiple ways. One way is to think along the following four dimensions: the physical dimension, the instructional dimension, the social/behavioral dimension, and the collaborative dimension.[27]

The chart on page 80, "Supplementary Aids and Services: Four Dimensions," expands on these. The guide may be used by the IEP Team or other professional staff, e.g. teachers, related services providers, etc.

The Blackline Master No. 11, page 81–83, "is a comprehensive listing of teacher-developed materials related to supplementary aids and services.

As part of its comprehensive redesign of special education services, and in an effort to provid inclusive opportunities for students with disabilities, the San Francisco Unified School District correlated some twenty common instructional strategies and modifications with the content standard areas the district has adopted and student learning styles. See pages 84–90.

A conceptual scheme developed at the Center for School and Community Integration identifies nine types of SAS adaptations.[28]

Size: Adapt the number of items that the learner is expected to learn or complete. For example, fewer comprehension questions for the student to complete.

Difficulty: Adapt the skill level or problem type. For example, ask questions that require only factual answers.

Input: Adapt the way instruction is delivered to the learner. For example, read the questions and discuss them before having students respond.

Output: Adapt how the student can respond to instruction. For example, permit the student to draw a picture or write a sentence that shows story comprehension.

Support: Increase the amount of personal assistance provided to the learner. For example, pair students and allow them to take turns answering.

Time: Adapt the time allotted and allowed for learning task completion, or testing. For example, provide the material to the student prior to the assignment being due or the test scheduled.

Degree of participation: Adapt the extent to which the learner is actively involved in the task. For example, involve the student in listening to the group discussion but do not require written comprehension questions.

Alternate goals: Adapt the goals or outcome expectations while using the same materials. For example, change the goal to listening for enjoyment; do not require comprehension questions.

Substitute curriculum: Provide different instruction and materials to meet a student's individual goals. For example, have the student find the date and time of favorite TV shows using the newspaper or TV Guide.

Anne M. Moll, formerly a specialist with the Kentucky State Education Department in the development of inclusive education programs and now a professor at Bellarmine College, has developed a three-step "hands-on" approach to addressing this challenge.

STEP 1: Know Your Students

The more the teacher knows about each student's interests, needs, and abilities, the better the match between curriculum, assessment and instruction, and actual learning. The following questions can serve as a guide in designing and implementing instruction.

- what are the interests of the student, both inside and outside of the classroom?

- what aspects of the language of instruction does the student understand?

- what aspects of the student's adaptive behavior impact learning?

- in what ways will physical aspects of the child interfere with typical access to learning?
- what background knowledge does the student have about the curriculum to be learned?
- what sensory-motor skills does the student have that might impact learning?
- what methods does the student use to learn?
- how can the student best demonstrate what s/he knows and can do?
- which specific learning strategies does the student use?

STEP 2: Determine the curriculum/content

Check your state, district, and school curriculum requirements and national standards for the field. Do not depend upon textbooks alone, unless the district has already aligned them with the state/national standards. No single text will meet the needs of all students. The following questions can serve as a guide in developing curriculum and content.

- what is the expected curriculum for this age/grade level? At the local/national levels?
- how are these expectations assessed?
- what are the expectations of previous knowledge in each curricular area?
- what skills are required?
- how were students prepared for this curricular level?
- what is the language used in the instruction?
- what problem solving skills are needed?
- what socialization skills are required.

STEP 3: Developing an instructional plan

Using the material developed regarding prior student knowledge and the curricular content, develop an instructional plan that takes into consideration the classroom and the "real world." The following questions can serve as a guide in developing the instructional plan.

Guiding questions:
- when and where will students use this information in the "real world"?
- why is it important for them to know this?
- what contexts will be appropriate for the student to use this knowledge?
- what methods will be used to assess student knowledge?
- what ways will the student demonstrate knowledge that reflects how the information will be used in the "real world"?

Three broad principles, derived from reports from school districts implementing inclusive education programs, can guide planning supplementary aids and services. They are:

1. Supplementary aids and services, while designed to address the needs of a particular child with a disability, provide benefit for all students, i.e., the classroom becomes a more effective environment for the learning of all.

2. Instructional strategies used in inclusive classrooms are practices recommended by educational researchers for students in general; as teachers report, "Good teaching is good teaching is good teaching."

3. In considering supplementary aids and services, they should be "only as special as necessary."[29]

This last point warrants amplification. In initial efforts to provide integrated opportunities for students with disabilities, there was a tendency to ensure success by providing maximal supports. That excess of help often became disabling rather than enabling. Too extensive adaptations are undesirable, in that they may unnecessarily single out the student with a disability, over-emphasize the student's differences and her/his need for adaptations, and separate or isolate the student from nondisabled classroom peers. The frequent practice of assigning an aide or paraprofessional to an individual student rather than to the class as a whole may result in the student becoming the responsibility of the aide, not the teacher. Zealous aides, in effect, may become "velcroed" to the student, separating her or him from classmates.

In providing any type of support it is essential to consider the preferences and reactions of the students themselves, particularly including the age- and cultural-appropriateness of the intervention. A study of social supports points to the gap between those strategies preferred by students and those conducted by teachers. The teachers leaned toward solving problems for the students rather than involving the students in the problem-solving. Teachers were more likely to focus on strategies that dealt with problem behaviors, conflict situations, and social and academic difficulties in the classroom, rather than using preventive strategies to foster social support, such as promoting respect, acceptance, and belonging where relationship-building and cooperative activities are encouraged.[30] Given the finding that as students with disabilities become older, their willingness and confidence in their ability to self-advocate declines, it is important that students at all grade levels are provided with opportunities to take responsibility for their own learning, and to learn the skills necessary to advocate for themselves and to address their own needs.

The phrase "natural supports" is used to describe those activities that are already present or at least readily available, that can be resources for the inclusion of students with disabilities, without being so special as to mitigate against membership in the class community. They are expanded below:

Natural supports: Resources for an inclusive classroom[31]

Staff members:

- Flexibility in role activities
- Role release
- Teaming and sharing
- Role clarification that encourages collaboration
- Use of classroom aides/paraprofessionals for class, not only for student(s) with disabilities.

Curriculum and instruction:

- Cooperative learning activities
- Infusion of disability-related topics as a regular part of the curriculum
- Modifications that are less obvious, which stand out less
- Activities that benefit disabled and nondisabled students alike.

Space:

- (Re)arrange space to benefit those with attention difficulties
- A cooling-off area/system, available to all students
- Random (and varied) assignment of students, disabled and nondisabled
- Opportunities for students to move about/leave the classroom without it being seen as a punishment.

Peers:

- Student assistance program available to all students
- Peer tutoring, making the classroom less teacher-centric
- Peer tutoring that rotates so as to enable students to be both tutor and tutee
- Cooperative learning activities.
- Activities that promote social networking.

A starting point for teachers in developing an instructional unit is the unit planning pyramid.[32] It allows the teacher to distinguish, for each subject area unit, what all students should learn, what most students should learn, and what some students should learn. The first category (the base of the pyramid) includes the most important concepts and is conceptually broader. The next category (the middle of the pyramid) represents the material of next greatest importance, e.g., additional facts, extension of base concepts, related concepts, more complex concepts. The last level (the top of the pyramid) may be considered supplemental material, more complex and/or more detailed. In thinking about each level, the teacher will need to consider the materials and resources needed, instructional strategies and adaptations, and evaluation and product outcomes. Given Gardner's concept of "jagged profiles" among students, i.e., strong in some areas and perhaps not so in others, as well as IDEA's requirement to recognize student differences subject-area-by-subject-area, individual students will fall in different segments of the pyramid for different subject areas.

In developing a program for an individual student with educational needs, teachers can consider a continuum of adaptations, from the least to the most significant adaptations.[33]

> *Least significant adaptations:* content remains the same; presentation and assessment may be slightly altered; examples include use of many visuals, preview-review lessons, use of cooperative groups, use of large print materials, use of peer coaching, giving students more time to complete tasks, use of amplification systems, student dictates responses to test/quiz questions, use of performance-based assessment.

> *Moderately significant adaptations:* standards stay the same or are slightly altered; more significant adaptations are made in presenting the lesson and in assessment; examples include use of taped lessons, changed sequence, smaller units, altered pace of instruction, off-level testing, reduced number and/or complexity of items, use of performance-based assessment.

> *Most significant adaptations:* major changes in standards; an expanded curriculum may be needed to include career/vocational and functional life skills: in some cases, an alternative curriculum is necessary; instructional techniques and assessment may involve use of assistive technology; examples include drawings to represent concepts, matching visual symbols with concepts, role playing, teacher observation, inventories, and use of communication boards.

While each student's program must be individual, and specified in her/his IEP, in broad terms one can expect that the great majority of students with disabilities will need the least significant adaptations.

In considering particular adaptations, teachers weigh factors such as:

- how much additional time and resources are required,
- whether the strategies will be effective,
- whether they will require significant changes in teaching/classroom environment,

- whether they are consistent with the teacher's philosophical orientation,

- whether the strategies are age-appropriate, unobtrusive, and perceived as fair, and

- how they will affect other students in the classroom.[34]

Extracurricular activities: Based on IDEA (and other federal legislation) a school district has obligations to provide curricular services to students with disabilities and to afford them the opportunity to participate in school-conducted or sponsored extracurricular activities. As in the academic area, participation may not be denied solely based upon the student's disability, the provision of supplementary aids and services is required. The activity, however, must not be so changed as to lose its integrity. There are many distinctions that schools need to consider: While there is no obligation for a school to waive competitive standards, thereby allowing a student who does not meet these standards to participate on the varsity basketball team, participation in an after-school intramural program is another matter.

What are accommodations and modifications "best practices" in assessment?

In of assessment, accommodations and modifications are not intended to give the student an unfair advantage. Rather, they enable students with a disability to demonstrate their knowledge without being impeded by their disability.

IDEA distinguishes among accommodations, modifications, and alternate assessment. "Accommodations" is used to define changes in format, response, setting, timing or scheduling that do not alter in a significant way what the test measures or the comparability of scores. In contrast, when changes in the assessment alter what the test is to measure or the comparability of scores, the term "modifications" is used. "Alternate assessment" is understood to mean an assessment designed for those students with disabilities who are unable to participate in general large-scale assessments used by a state or district, even when accommodations or modifications are used.[35] The preponderance of students with disabilities will participate in assessments either without any adaptations or with accommodations. By national standards, fewer than ten percent of students with disabilities will need the most significant adaptations.

Some principles that can guide the determination of accommodations and modifications include:

- accommodations or modifications are not needed by every student with a disability,

- accommodations/modification should be determined specific to each subject area,

- accommodations/modifications must be determined by the IEP Team. (While the IEP Team has the authority to determine the needed accommodation/modification, some states[36] (and districts) have lists of officially approved accommodations. These should be consulted as part of IEP Team's determination),

- accommodations/modifications should be integrated into classroom instruction,

- accommodations/modification must not compromise the intent of the assessment,

- only those accommodations/modifications that are needed should be used.

The requirement that students with disabilities participate in district- and state-wide assessments is in keeping with IDEA's focus on student learning outcomes. Whether that participation involves the use of accommodations, modifications, or alternate assessments, the scores of students with disabilities are to be aggregated with the scores of all other students, as well as disaggregated. The aggregated scores emphasize the "whole school" approach to the education of students with disabilities, making their outcomes a part of the school's results. The disaggregated scores allow for identifying more specific outcomes for students with disabilities, precluding their being masked in an overall average. While this IDEA requirement is at the state level, increasing numbers of states and local districts are extending the reporting of scores to the performance of their students with disabilities. Indeed, this pattern of reporting has become a part of many national reform proposals.

Accommodations and modifications may be grouped into the following categories:

Timing: changes in duration
- extended time
- frequent breaks

Scheduling: changes in when the activity occurs
- over several days
- at a particular time of the day
- changed order to sub-tests

Setting: changes in the location

- preferential seating (i.e., a particular place in the classroom)
- separate location
- specialized setting (i.e., with noise buffers, special lighting, etc.)

Presentation: changes in how material is given

- Braille, large print, large answer bubbles, fewer items per page)
- read test and/or directions
- reread instructions
- cues (e.g., highlighting key words or phrases, symbol cues)
- prompts
- clarification (e.g., explain the directions, provide extra examples)
- templates (e.g., mask part of the page, yet to be addressed or already completed)
- markers (i.e., assist student in identifying place in text)
- magnifying and/or amplification devices

Response: changes in how a student can demonstrate knowledge

- student marking in test booklet (instead of on answer form)
- use of a scribe to record answers
- fewer choices in a multiple choice test
- provide examples prior to formal testing
- verbal response
- pencil grips
- special paper (i.e., allows aligning responses)
- math tools (e.g., number lines, arithmetic tables, manipulatives, calculators)
- reference materials (e.g., dictionaries, vocabulary bank, spell checkers)
- technology (respond on a computer)
- point to answer.

Grading

While the reauthorized IDEA specifically addresses participation of students with disabilities in state- and district-wide assessment programs, it does not address the matter of student grading. In the absence of direction from the federal law, decisions as to grading need to be made in the context of state and district policies. Tomlinson makes the cogent point that grading practices should grow from a philosophy of teaching and learning that respects students' differences and reflects individual growth.[37] Looking at grading from her perspective as a teacher, she proposes the following:

- student's success must reflect the degree of his/her own growth,

- the grade for a student's work should be on the basis of clearly delineated criteria for the particular work assignment,

- grading should provide consistent and meaningful feedback to the student that clarifies present successes and next learning steps,

- report grades should reflect growth patterns,

- on report cards, parents should be able to see both individual student growth and relative standing.[38]

An overall guiding principal can be discerned from IDEA's emphasis on mastery of the regular curriculum and a presumption for services to be provided in the general education environment. It is possible to have standards and inclusion. Students with disabilities served in the general education classroom should be graded in a manner consistent with that for their nondisabled peers when appropriate. As schools have increased inclusive practices, many alternative grading approaches have been developed that are used for all students. They can be used by teachers in a classroom alone or by those who collaborate with another teacher. Salend describes a number of different alternative grading schemes. They appear below.

Grading Schemes

IEP grading: Grade determined in the context of the student meeting her/his IEP goals.

Student self-comparison: Based upon teacher and student agreement as to goals, grade is determined based upon progress toward meeting them.

Contract grading: Per an agreed upon "contract" between teacher(s) and student,
that specifies outcomes, products to demonstrate mastery, evaluation strategies, and time lines.

Pass/fail: Mastery of material receives a "pass" grade.

Mastery level/criterion systems: Per particular learning activities, mastery levels are determined and their achievement measured.

Checklists: Similar to mastery standards.

Multiple grading: Grades for different factors, such as ability, achievement, and effort.

Level grading: A subscript denotes the level of difficulty upon which the grade was based.

Descriptive grading: Teachers provide descriptive comments assessing student achievement.[39]

Where can I find additional information regarding differentiated classrooms, supplementary aids and services, accommodations and modifications?

The concept of a differentiated or student-focused classroom builds upon the work of many practitioners, researchers, and theoreticians, especially the work of Carol Ann Tomlinson. Supplementary aids and services and modifications are addressed in a myriad of sources. Some of them are noted below.

Bauder, A. M. & Shea, T. M. (1999). *Inclusion 101: How to teach all learners.* Baltimore, MD: Paul H. Brookes Publishing Co.

Cole, S., Horvath, B., Chapman, C., Deschenes, C. Ebeling, D. G., & Sprague, J. (2000). *Adapting curriculum and instruction in the inclusive classroom: A teacher's desk reference*, 2nd ed. Bloomington, IN: The Center for School and Community Integration, Institute for the Study of Developmental Disabilities.

Heron, E. & Joregensen, C. M. (1995). Addressing differences right from the start. *Educational Leadership*, 54(4), 56–58.

Hoerr, T. (2000). *The Mutiple Intelligences School*. Alexandria, VA: Association for School and Curriculum Development. See also, www.newcityschool.org.

Making assessment accommodations: A toolkit for educators (2000). Reston, VA: Council for Exceptional Children.

Meyer, A. & O'Neil, L. M. (June 2000). Supporting the motivation to learn: How universal design for learning can help. *Exceptional Parent Magazine*, 35–39.

Questions and answers about provisions in the Individuals with Disabilities Education Act Amendments of 1997 related to students with disabilities and state and district-wide assessments (August 24, 2000). Washington, DC: Office of Special Education and Rehabilitative Services, US Department of Education.

Tomlinson, C. A. (September 2000). Reconcilable differences? Standards-based teaching and differentiation. *Educational Leadership*, 58(1), 6–11.

Tomlinson, C. A. (1999). *The differentiated classroom: Responding to the needs of all learners* . Alexandria, VA: Association for Supervision and Curriculum Development.

Tomlinson, C. A. (1995). *How to differentiate instruction in mixed ability classrooms*. Alexandria, VA: Association for Supervision and Curriculum Development.

Tomlinson, C.A. (1997). *Differentiating instruction: Facilitators guide*. Alexandria, VA: Association for Supervision and Curriculum Development.

Udvari-Solner, A. (1995). A process for adapting curriculum in inclusive classrooms. In R. A. Villa & J. Thousand (Eds.), *Creating an inclusive school* (pp. 110–124). Alexandria, VA: Association for Supervision and Curriculum Development.

THE MULTIPLE INTELLIGENCES TABLE

Intelligence	What Is It?	Students Like To	Teachers Can
Interpersonal	• Sensitive to the feelings and moods of others. • Understands and interacts effectively with others.	• Enjoy many friends. • Lead, share, mediate. • Build consensus and empathize with others. • Work as an effective team member.	• Use cooperative learning. • Assign group projects. • Give students opportunities for peer teaching. • Brainstorm solutions to problems. • Create situations in which students are given feedback from others.
Intrapersonal	• Sensitive to one's own feelings and moods. • Knows own strengths and weaknesses. • Uses self-knowledge to guide decision-making and set goals.	• Control own feelings and moods. • Pursue personal interests and set individual agendas. • Learn through observing and listening. • Use metacognigive skills.	• Allow students to work at own pace. • Assign individual, self-directed projects. • Help students set goals. • Provide opportunities for students to get feedback from each other. • Involve the students in journal writing and other forms of reflection.
Bodily-Kinesthetic	• Uses one's body to communicate and solve problems. • Is adept with objects and activities involving fine or gross motor skills.	• Play sports and be physically active. • Use body language. • Do crafts and mechanical projects. • Dance, act or mime.	• Provide tactile and movement activities. • Offer role playing and acting opportunities. • Involve the students in physical activity. • Allow the students to move while working.
Linguistic	• Thinks in words. • Uses language and words in many different forms to express complex meanings.	• Tell jokes, riddles or puns. • Read, write or tell stories. • Use an expanded vocabulary. • Play word games. • Create poems and stories using the sounds and imagery of words.	• Use sewing, model-making and other activities using fine motor skills. • Create reading and writing projects. • Help the students prepare speeches. • Interest the students in debates. • Make word games, crossword puzzles and word searches. • Encourage the use of puns, palindromes and outrageous words.

Created by faculty of the New City School, 1996, and found in *Succeeding with Multiple Intelligences: Teaching Through the Personal Intelligences;* editors Sally Boggeman, Tom Hoerr, and Christine Wallach. *www.newcityschool.org*

THE MULTIPLE INTELLIGENCES TABLE (continued)

Intelligence	What Is It?	Students Like To	Teachers Can
Logical-Mathematical	• Approaches problems logically. • Understands number and abstract patterns. • Recognizes and solves problems using reasoning skills.	• Work with numbers, figure things out and analyze situations. • Know how things work. • Ask questions. • Exhibit precision in problem solving. • Work in situations in which there are clear black and white solutions.	• Construct Venn diagrams. • Use games of strategy. • Have students demonstrate understanding using concrete objects. • Record information on graphs. • Establish time lines and draw maps.
Musical	• Sensitive to non-verbal sounds in the enfironment, including melody and tone. • Aware of patterns in rhythm, pitch and timbre.	• Listen to and play music. • Match feelings tomusic and rhythms. • Sing, hum and move to music. • Remember and work with different musical forms. • Create and replicate tunes.	• Rewrite song lyrics to teach a concept. • Encourage students to add music to plays. • Create musical mnemonics. • Teach history through music of the period. • Have studnets learn music and folk dancing from other countries.
Naturalist	• Sensitive to the natural world. • Sees connections and patterns within the plant and animal kingdoms.	• Spend time outdoors. • Observe plants, collect rocks and try to catch animals. • Listen to the sounds created in the natural world. • Notice relationships in nature.Categorize and classify flora and fauna.	• Use the outdoors as a classroom. • Have plants and animals in the classroom for which students are responsible. • Conduct hands-on science experiments. • Create a nature area on the playground.
Spatial	• Perceives the visual world accurately. • Creates mental images. • Thinks three-dimensionally. • Aware of relationship between objects in space.	• Doodle, paint, draw or create threedimensional representations. • Look at maps. • Work puzzles or complete mazes. • Take things apart and put them back together.	• Draw maps and mazes. • Lead visualization activities. • Provide opportunities to show understanding through drawing or painting. • Have students design clothing, buildings, play areas and scenery.

Created by faculty of the New City School, 1996, and found in *Succeeding with Multiple Intelligences: Teaching Through the Personal Intelligences;* editors Sally Boggeman, Tom Hoerr, and Christine Wallach. *www.newcityschool.org*

SUPPLEMENTARY AIDS AND SERVICES: FOUR DIMENSIONS.

Below is a list of suggestions related to four dimensions of supplementary aids and services. Space has been provided for you to add your own ideas.

1. *Physical dimension:*
   - Could the classroom be made more accessible for the student?
   - Could a different size/shape table be available for small group work?
   - Does the student need to be specially positioned?
   - _____

2. *Instructional dimension:*
   - Does the student need visual aids, large print, alternative media?
   - Could the student be provided reading guides or tape-recorded texts?
   - Could the student be allowed extra time for completion of assignments, have shortened assignments, be provided with a calculator or word processor?
   - Could the student have take home or oral tests? Could the student use a study guide during tests? Could tests be shortened? Divided in parts to be taken over an extended period of time?
   - Could the student be graded pass/fail? Or receive IEP progress grading?
   - Could cooperative learning or reciprocal teaching be used? Could a partner be assigned?
   - Could the student work on related activities?
   - Could the student work on alternative skills?
   - Could the student be provided computer-assisted instruction, communication switches or software? Does the student require electronic aids or services?
   - _____

3. *Social/behavioral dimension:*
   - Could the student be involved in social skill instruction?
   - Does the student need counseling?
   - Does the student need a behavior management plan?
   - Could the student use self-monitoring of target behaviors?
   - Could peers be used to monitor and/or redirect behavior? Could peers provide instructional assistance?
   - Could group support activities be initiated?
   - _____

4. *Collaborative dimension:*
   - Does the student require assistance from a paraprofessional or aide? On an individual basis? For what activities?
   - Does the student need additional strategy or study skill training?
   - Could the teacher(s) receive assistance from a curriculum consultant, instructional specialists, behavior specialist?
   - Could the student be served in a classroom staffed by a regular and special educator? If so, how would this be organized? How will the teachers plan and work together?
   - _____

SUPPLEMENTARY AIDS & SERVICES: TEACHER DEVELOPED EXAMPLES

The following are examples of supplementary aids and services that support student learning. They have been compiled by the authors from teachers with whom they have worked.

Modify the environment:
- seat students in the classroom according to needs (e.g., attention, hearing, vision, behaviors),
- assign seats to students with audiology deficits away from noise,
- reduce visual distractions,
- ensure adequate ventilation,
- limit oral distractions (i.e., noise),
- consider using workspace other than student's desk,
- establish a daily routine, and post the daily schedule,
- clear student's work area of unnecessary/distracting material.

Modify the pace:
- reduce or substitute assignments,
- minimize recopying tasks,
- minimize copying tasks when a word or phrase will do,
- allow breaks,
- vary activities,
- allow additional time to preview materials, complete tasks, review material,
- use a timer to indicate pace.

Modify the materials used in the classroom:
- fold or line paper to help students who have problems spatially or need organizational structure,
- utilize different types of paper,
- use a whiteboard for easier vision,
- reduce excess paper/other materials on desk so that the student will not be distracted,
- use grip on pen/pencil for students with handwriting problems,
- use highlighting or color coding for directions, key words, topic sentences, summary, etc.,
- tape record directions/assignments,
- read written questions/directions aloud,
- complete first problem as example,
- reduce the amount of material on the page,
- allow students to use a word processor for writing and editing,
- allow students to use a calculator,
- shorten the length of the assignment,
- tape written materials, so that the students can follow along with reading,
- outline reading material,
- read/tape record tests/quizzes,
- use manipulatives and other physical objects.

(continued on next page)

Structure study skills:
- have students keep an assignment book, with special page(s) for homework,
- provide a daily or weekly homework assignment list,
- vary the assignment for the same objective,
- ask students to repeat directions in own words,
- return corrected assignments with specific comments, as quickly as possible,
- break down assignments into smaller units,
- provide advanced due dates for long term assignments, along with interim deadlines,
- allow students opportunities to provide sample responses,
- teach test-taking skills, e.g., which problems to do first, process of elimination, signal words/directive words,
- teach skimming/scanning skills,
- teach use of table of contents, index, chapter heading, subunit headings, glossary,
- teach previewing skills, questions to ask prior to reading text,
- provide vocabulary lists,
- encourage peer assistance/cooperative learning,
- establish home/school communication system for completion of assignment, upcoming matters,
- provide varied activities for a given concept.

Modify instructional methods:
- use a multi-sensory approach to presenting material,
- consider varied student learning styles when presenting material,
- test orally,
- read test questions,
- use concrete objects/examples to demonstrate concepts,
- provide structure for students to classify information, e.g., outlines, study guides, graphic organizers, webs,
- have students restate/paraphrase information/directions,
- teach students to organize their paperwork/work space,
- do not penalize for handwriting/spelling when these are not the subject of the lesson,
- provide student information at her/his desk when copying from the board is a problem,
- simplify directions, and make them brief,
- allow students to dictate responses to a teacher, peer, or tape recorder,
- display sample of finished products along with directions and materials used,
- allow time at the beginning of the lesson to review previous knowledge in relationship to the new lesson. Allow time at the end to summarize,
- ask factual questions and then turn to inferential questioning,
- testing broken into segments, and use of oral testing,
- vocabulary available before unit is introduced,
- provide essential fact(s) list,
- provide discussion questions prior to reading,
- block out confusing worksheets,

(continued on next page)

- provide transition directions,
- teach and cue key direction words,
- segment directions,
- provide guided practice,
- provide practice trials,
- during the lesson, provide an overview of the material to be presented (e.g., advanced organizers), visual material, interject hands-on tasks, use voice change to stress points, repeat important information, use humor to keep attention, have students orally summarize key points, circulate around the room, model activity desired,
- use large print,
- provide context for the new material,
- use student's prior knowledge both to access and extend the lesson,
- validate the student's past experience/knowledge.

Modify presentation:
- establish a rationale for learning,
- use student's name incorporated into the question,
- incorporate popular themes/characters,
- provide functional link to material,
- ask frequent questions,
- change question level,
- use hand signals to cue behavior,
- alter sequence of presentation,
- repeat major points,
- use verbal cues, e.g., list or number key points, note that which is important,
- change tone of voice,
- provide anticipation cues,
- provide mnemonic devices.

Testing:
- ask oral multiple choice questions,
- organize test from easy to hard,
- enlarge or highlight key words on test items,
- change response format,
- alter objective criterion level,
- adapt test items for differing response modes,
- use timer to show allocated time.

Inclusion: A Service, Not A Place, Alan Gartner and Dorothy Kerzner Lipsky.

MATRIX OF INSTRUCTIONAL STRATEGIES AND MODIFICATIONS FOR ADDRESSING INDIVIDUAL LEARNING NEEDS & STYLES (LISTED ALPHABETICALLY BY NAME OF ACTIVITY)

The materials that follow were provided by the san Francisco Unified School District, 1999. Reprinted with permission.

Content Standard Area	Strategy/Modification	Need Areas Addressed	Additional Modifications	Learning Styles
✓ LA-reading ✓ LA-writing ✓ LA-oral ✓ Math ✓ Science ✓ Hist./Soc. St.	**Active Note Taking**—Students divide a piece of paper in half. On one side record notes from reading; on the other write comments questions, or reactions.	• Putting ideas together • Selecting key points • Support for reluctant speakers • Focused comprehension • Idea generalization • Organizational skills	• Provide written prompts or questions for students having difficulty generating their own ideas • Partner work • Additional extension questions for GATE • Provide computer template with key words, categories, or phrases	Linguistic Logical Intrapersonal
✓ LA-reading ✓ LA-writing ✓ LA-oral ✓ Math ✓ Science ✓ Hist./Soc. St.	**"Author's" Chair**—Provide regular opportunities for individual students to share a product or assignment with rest of the class or within a small group (writing, read aloud, solve a problem, explain a procedure). Provide all students with an opportunity over time. The audience is encouraged to participate with questions, responses.	• Clarify of identify key process steps • Informal assessment of student understanding or application • Language expression • Auditory support for audience • Sequencing • Student self-assessment	• Allow some students to work with a partner • Work can be "in process" or finished • Allow for different modes of presentation • Allow or require shorter or longer presentation time • Provide audience with guiding questions for comprehension, language development, focus on key information • Video or audio tape student participation	Linguistic Logical Interpersonal Intrapersonal
✓ LA-reading ✓ LA-writing ✓ LA-oral ✓ Math ✓ Science ✓ Hist./Soc. St.	**Brainstorming**—Engage students in brainstorming before they begin to read a selection. Write all words and concepts on board or chart (e.g. possible ways to solve a problem, do a procedure, cause effect, predictions). Tell them to read to see if their ideas are reflected in the text.	• Attention, focus • Idea generation, fluency • Vocabulary development • Sequencing • Focused guide for reading • Key reference points • Making personal connections • Connecting to previous learning	• Record words on cards or in a personal dictionary (ELL) • Make a form on which students can record or have another student record the ideas to support visual/motor difficulties (SLD) • Make large copies and post as a reference (ELL, SLD) • Provide templates with key words or phrases to help students record ideas	Linguistic Spatial Interpersonal Intrapersonal

MATRIX OF INSTRUCTIONAL STRATEGIES AND MODIFICATIONS FOR ADDRESSING INDIVIDUAL LEARNING NEEDS & STYLES (LISTED ALPHABETICALLY BY NAME OF ACTIVITY)

Content Standard Area	Strategy/Modification	Need Areas Addressed	Additional Modifications	Learning Styles
✓ LA-reading ✓ LA-writing ✓ LA-oral ✓ Math ✓ Science ✓ Hist/Soc. St.	**Double Entry Journal**—Students divide a sheet of paper in half. On the left side readers identify a passage or quotation of significance in the selection. On the right side, they write their responses, questions, connections, reflections about the passage.	• Language expression • Idea expansion • Key concept identification format for responding to reading • Connect to personal experiences	• Identify key words, concepts, or passages and prepare in advance to focus learner (at-risk, SLD) • Limited or extend the number of required entries • Use to record important/key concepts from text read • Add section for vocabulary (ELL, SLD at-risk) • Use tables in "word" software to create half of the entries with the learner developing the questions	Linguistic Logical Spatial Kinesthetic Intrapersonal
✓ LA-reading ✓ LA-writing ✓ LA-oral ✓ Math ✓ Science ✓ Hist/Soc. St.	**Expert Group**—(Similar to Jigsaw or Retrieval Charts). Students work in a small group in one area being studied and teach it to other groups. (e.g. expert in one character of a story, historical figure, event, organ, system, etc.)	• Limit/focus area of study • Manage large blocks of information • Taking individual responsibility • Using peer support • Organizing information • Information processing	• Allow for student choice, or to work in an area of strength • Assigned roles for group work • Peer or partner support • Adjust for time needed to complete the task • Provide extended categories or details (GATE) • Additional language experience or vocabulary (ELL)	Linguistic Logical Spatial Musical Kinesthetic Interpersonal Intrapersonal
✓ LA-reading ✓ LA-writing ✓ LA-oral ✓ Math ✓ Science ✓ Hist/Soc. St.	**Focused Question**—When correcting or reviewing student work, let them know that you will be looking for one key feature such as use of descriptive words, subject-verb agreement, steps in a procedure, showing steps in problem solving, etc.	• Attention • Understanding and applying key concepts • Processing information	• Read or show samples from individual student work daily. Focus on key skill or process. • Critique samples of work with whole class or small group	Linguistic Logical Spatial

MATRIX OF INSTRUCTIONAL STRATEGIES AND MODIFICATIONS FOR ADDRESSING INDIVIDUAL LEARNING NEEDS & STYLES (LISTED ALPHABETICALLY BY NAME OF ACTIVITY)

Content Standard Area	Strategy/Modification	Need Areas Addressed	Additional Modifications	Learning Styles
✓ LA-reading ✓ LA-writing ✓ LA-oral ✓ Math ✓ Science ✓ Hist/Soc. St.	**Graphic Organizers**—Use story maps, charts, graphs, character maps, fishbone, Venn diagrams, mind maps, retrieval charts. Use these visual representation of new ideas, review, or to depict information from text read.	• Generate ideas • Expressive language • Organization • Memory • Making connections • Adding detail • Patterns/relationships • Abstract thinking (GATE)	• Use a tape recorder for students who benefit from auditory input • Working with a partner to build language, assist with organization or ideas • Word walls or personal dictionaries for ELL • Use software such as Inspiration to develop outlines/organizational charts	Linguistic Logical Spatial Kinesthetic Intrapersonal
✓ LA-reading ✓ LA-writing ✓ LA-oral ✓ Math ✓ Science ✓ Hist/Soc. St.	**Give One, Get One**—Students list all of the information they know about a specific topic on a sheet of paper. Each student then shares his/her list with at least two other students. As they share, they add one new thing they learn from the other person. The class as a whole then shares lists and teacher or students record facts/information on overhead for class to copy.	• Visual and auditory reinforcement • Memory • Idea generation • Vocabulary development • Making connections • Patterns/relationships	• Teacher can make a final copy for students who may have difficulty (SLD) • Give students the transparency to copy if it is difficult to do from a distance • Share in small groups if attention and movement are difficult for student • Provide specific, guiding questions to focus the generation of ideas	Linguistic Logical Spatial Kinesthetic Musical Interpersonal Intrapersonal
✓ LA-reading ✓ LA-writing ✓ LA-oral ✓ Math ✓ Science ✓ Hist/Soc. St.	**Group Investigation Model**—Students work in cooperative groups. Teacher gives group open-ended discussion questions about a text selection. Students discuss questions, come to consensus and write the answers or present them orally.	• Auditory support • Focus and memory • Vocabulary and concept expansion and acquisition • Self-expression • Active thinking • Making choices or connections	• Teacher monitors or works with individuals or small groups to guide or support the work • Have representative of group report the group response • Use to support problem solving or process work • Assigned peer or partner support • Provide specific rules such as one idea expressed by each student to encourage individual participation	Linguistic Logical Spatial Interpersonal Intrapersonal

MATRIX OF INSTRUCTIONAL STRATEGIES AND MODIFICATIONS FOR ADDRESSING INDIVIDUAL LEARNING NEEDS & STYLES (LISTED ALPHABETICALLY BY NAME OF ACTIVITY)

Content Standard Area	Strategy/Modification	Need Areas Addressed	Additional Modifications	Learning Styles
✓ LA-reading ✓ LA-writing ✓ LA-oral ✓ Math ✓ Science ✓ Hist/Soc. St.	**Interactive Journals**—On one half of a page, the student records notes, key ideas, concepts, concerns, events, connections, procedures from content class. On the other half of the page, the teacher responds with questions, comments, praise, suggestions.	• Receiving and using suggestions and help focus and reinforce key concepts • Memory support • Decision making • Making personal questions • Expanding thinking	• Provide journals to students with predetermined questions, format, size • Adapt size and shape and methods of responses to address individual student needs • Create a list of available questions or prompts to which students can choose or be assigned to respond	Linguistic Logical Spatial Kinesthetic Intrapersonal
✓ LA-reading ✓ LA-writing ✓ LA-oral ✓ Math ✓ Science ✓ Hist/Soc. St.	**KWL**—Model active thinking in the reading of expository text. At the beginning of a lesson, the teacher asks students, as a group, what they already know about a topic. Teacher records the responses. What questions do they want answered or information they want to learn? Can the information be grouped or clustered in any way. After reading or discussion, the students record what they learned.	• Active thinking • Idea generation • Experience building • Connecting to student experiences and prior knowledge • Vocabulary development • Memory support • Visual and auditory support • Preview-readiness for learning	• Use an overhead or chart paper to record responses. Post for reference. • Provide forms on which students can record the information, take notes • Students can work with a partner or in small group to determine what was learned at the end of the lesson • Keep personal dictionary or word list for vocabulary building • Allow extra time for completion • Identify number of responses that are necessary • Do manageable chunks of material at a time	Linguistic Logical Spatial Kinesthetic Musical Interpersonal Intrapersonal
✓ LA-reading ✓ LA-writing ✓ LA-oral ✓ Math ✓ Science ✓ Hist/Soc. St.	**Literature Circles**—Small, temporary groups of students that meet on a regular schedule to discuss their reading. Each group may choose or be assigned a different book to read, based on interest or reading level.	• Engage reluctant readers • Connect to personal experiences and interests • Build auditory capacity and listening skills • Oral expression • Check for understanding • Flexible use of time or comprehension focus	• Provide limited and/or focused questions to assist students in guiding their reading or for discussion • Allow choices of topics/questions discussed (GATE, ELL, SLD) • Provide a variety of book types and levels to accommodate reading skills of students • Use a variety of levels of supplementary reading materials to support learning in content areas	Linguistic Logical Interpersonal Intrapersonal

MATRIX OF INSTRUCTIONAL STRATEGIES AND MODIFICATIONS FOR ADDRESSING INDIVIDUAL LEARNING NEEDS & STYLES (LISTED ALPHABETICALLY BY NAME OF ACTIVITY)

Content Standard Area	Strategy/Modification	Need Areas Addressed	Additional Modifications	Learning Styles
✓ LA-reading ✓ LA-writing ✓ LA-oral ✓ Math ✓ Science ✓ Hist/Soc. St.	**Manipulative and Visual Prompts**—Provide support tools for students in the form of markers, color coded pages, folders, highlighters, post-it notes, reading markers, counting markers, or other manipulatives that assist them in focusing on, organizing, or understanding their work.	• Support visual learning • Focus on key items, words, concepts • Provide opportunities to work with "hands-on" materials • Organization • Memory	• Encourage students to select their own way of organizing their work • Use computer generated organizers or visual tools • Create consistent formats to assist students in organizing their ideas • Allow students generate their own designs or patterns for identifying key ideas	Linguistic Logical Spatial Kinesthetic Intrapersonal
✓ LA-reading ✓ LA-writing ✓ LA-oral ✓ Math ✓ Science ✓ Hist/Soc. St.	**Project Cube**—A project cube is a way to visually present information about a book, text, or other source of content information. On the six sides of the cube, students put words and/or pictures that will tell others about the information learned by the student.	• Summarization • Visualize • Vocabulary development • Making choices • Making connections • Multiple modalities • Focus, selection of key ideas	• Encourage students to use a variety of representations of content knowledge including drawing, music, metaphor, oral presentations, etc. • Make cubes in advance for students as needed. Add questions or key topic on each side • Provide examples and models ad reference point.	Linguistic Logical Spatial Musical Kinesthetic Intrapersonal
✓ LA-reading ✓ LA-writing ✓ LA-oral ✓ Math ✓ Science ✓ Hist/Soc. St.	**Questions First**—Provide questions or step by step directions for an assignment PRIOR to asking students to read or listen. This provides a preparation, readiness, and context for listening or reading.	• Limited focus • Preview • Attention • Comprehension • Order sequencing	• Provide a graphic organizer in advance to help students focus and organize • Adjust type and/or number of questions a student is to answer • Provide choices in how answer or information is to be represented to demonstrate understanding	Linguistic Logical Spatial Intrapersonal
✓ LA-reading ✓ LA-writing ✓ LA-oral ✓ Math ✓ Science ✓ Hist/Soc. St.	**Quick Write**—At key points in a class discussion, procedure, or presentation, students are asked to stop and to a "quick write." This allows students to think about what they have read, heard, or seen and respond to it in their own words. They can include questions or make predictions about what will happen next.	• Clarify thinking • Check comprehension • Use key vocabulary and concepts • Use writing to reinforce reading or listening • Memory reinforcement • Organization	• Create an ongoing and consistent format for Quick Write such as journal, learning log, math or science notebook • Allow for revisions or revisits, or sharing with others • Allow for graphic representation or drawing • Record responses on tape • Use stop and "speak" instead of writing	Linguistic Logical Spatial Kinesthetic Intrapersonal

MATRIX OF INSTRUCTIONAL STRATEGIES AND MODIFICATIONS FOR ADDRESSING INDIVIDUAL LEARNING NEEDS & STYLES (LISTED ALPHABETICALLY BY NAME OF ACTIVITY)

Content Standard Area	Strategy/Modification	Need Areas Addressed	Additional Modifications	Learning Styles
✓ LA-reading LA-writing LA-oral ✓ Math ✓ Science ✓ Hist/Soc. St.	**Reciprocal Reading**—Students take turns reading with a partner. At periodic intervals, the listener asks the reader key questions about what was read, such as identifying main idea, summarizing, clarifying, or predicting. Teacher models with students first, then students work in pairs.	• Expressive language • Memory • Information processing • Sequencing • Vocabulary building • Auditory processing • Summarizing	• Use shorter passages for reading if needed • Have a third group member generate questions if it is too difficult for one student to do • Write answers for memory and reinforcement	Linguistic Logical Spatial Intrapersonal
✓ LA-reading LA-writing LA-oral ✓ Math ✓ Science ✓ Hist/Soc. St.	**"Relic" Box**—Items related to a specific character, setting, event, topic, or process are placed in a box or bag. The teacher pulls the items from the box one at a time and asks students to predict what it tells them about what will be read or studied. What will happen? What might they learn?	• Experience, language building • Concrete connection to abstract ideas • Making connections • Inference • Attention, focus • Reinforce auditory skills • Kinesthetic and visual modalities	• Students can create their own relic boxed following a book read or at the completion of a unit of student • Use real or representational object • Allow students to see and touch the objects up close	Linguistic Logical Spatial Musical Kinesthetic Interpersonal Intrapersonal
✓ LA-reading LA-writing LA-oral ✓ Math ✓ Science ✓ Hist/Soc. St.	**Storyboard**—Have students visually recall or represent major events of a story or chapter. Students use blank copies of a storyboard that has been divided into sections representing the major events, chapters, headings, time periods, etc. Students illustrate in sequence or by heading, the events or key information. Students share storyboard with others.	• Clarify thinking • Sequence • Organizing and classifying • Support and build visual, spatial, and kinesthetic skills • Focus • Identify key ideas • Multiple representations • Reinforcement of ideas	• Prepare a large, class example to serve as a model. Add or reduce number of squares. • Label or identify the types of content to be included • Have students work with a partner or in a small group for support, added ideas, help • Encourage variety of depictions— written, drawn, cut pictures, words, clusters, etc. • Use *Inspiration, Power Point,* or a draw program for students to plan their writing or presentation • Assign one topic or square to each member of a group rather than a complete storyboard for each student	Linguistic Logical Spatial Intrapersonal

MATRIX OF INSTRUCTIONAL STRATEGIES AND MODIFICATIONS FOR ADDRESSING INDIVIDUAL LEARNING NEEDS & STYLES (LISTED ALPHABETICALLY BY NAME OF ACTIVITY)

Content Standard Area	Strategy/Modification	Need Areas Addressed	Additional Modifications	Learning Styles
✓ LA-reading LA-writing ✓ LA-oral ✓ Math ✓ Science ✓ Hist/Soc. St.	**Think Aloud**—The teacher models some of the thinking processes that a good reader engages in when reading. The teacher reads to the students as they follow along with their own copy. The teacher stops throughout the reading to model self-reflection, questioning. Why did the character do this? Why might they act that way? Why was she angry? What might happen next? How do I know? What step do you think will follow? How did I reach this conclusion?	• Information processing • Auditory processing and reinforcement • Check for understanding • Modeling • Verbalization • Vocabulary development • Making connections • Making inferences, applying knowledge	• Students can listen to story or chapter on tape with thinking processes and questions modeled periodically throughout • Students can re-listen to the tape • Use video in the same manner • Students can practice with a partner asking questions • Have a prepared list of questions that can be asked as student reads • Allow sufficient time for student responses, use partners • Tape student reading and personal discussion	Linguistic Logical Musical Interpersonal Intrapersonal
✓ LA-reading LA-writing ✓ LA-oral ✓ Math ✓ Science ✓ Hist/Soc. St.	**Think-Pair-Share**—Provide students with a question or problem, or reading that is to be analyzed. Ask them to read or think about the answer individually. Share their answer or thoughts with a partner. Agree upon a key idea, answer, or explanation, then share with others in another group or whole class.	• Auditory processing • Listening practice • Identify key concepts • Verbalization • Applying information • Check for understanding • Language development	• Provide a consistent time limit to allow time for each person to share and respond to thinking • Extend time for some students • Allow for responses other than verbally	Linguistic Logical Spatial Interpersonal Intrapersonal

San Francisco Unified School District, 1999, Printed with permission.

6

Cooperative Learning and Peer Supports

Just for the fun of it: Test yourself on your current knowledge of cooperative learning and peer supports.

What are the different types of cooperative learning?

_____

_____

Turn to page 93 to read about this topic.

How do cooperative learning programs serve students of diverse abilities?

_____

_____

Turn to page 93 to read about this topic.

How do cooperative learning programs relate to the regular activities of the general education classroom?

_____

_____

Turn to page 94 to read about this topic.

What are different types of peer supports?

_____

_____

Turn to page 95 to read about this topic.

What are the benefits of peer supports? For which students?

_____

_____

Turn to page 96 to read about this topic.

Which students can be providers of peer supports?

_____

_____

Turn to page 96 to read about this topic.

What is cooperative learning?

Cooperative learning enables students, including those with disabilities, to be involved in and benefit from the school's instructional program. Cooperative learning is more than putting students into small groups. It shifts the roles of both the students and the teachers. Students become more active participants and less passive recipients, while teachers take on more of a role of coach or facilitator. Cooperative learning may be considered a supplementary aid and service; it was selected by teachers in the NCERI study as the most important instructional tool in support of inclusive education. Cooperative learning warrants special attention for the following additional reasons:

- there is a strong research base as to its positive outcomes for both general and special education students,
- there is a well-developed body of literature on its implementation across classrooms, grade levels, and subject matter,
- it is commonly used in general education classrooms and familiar to regular education teachers,
- it is the most frequently used strategy in general education classrooms with special education students, i.e., inclusive classrooms,
- it actively engages each of the students, in different roles,
- its design is intrinsically inclusive.

There are several different designs of cooperative learning. Some serve as an adjunct within a broader curricula framework while, in other designs, cooperative learning is a key feature of a comprehensive reform plan. Common to all of the programs that have shown significant gains for students are two complementary features: promoting interdependence within the groups, by having the partners work together to accomplish the goal; and holding students individually accountable for demonstrating their mastery of the knowledge or skill. Each design considers interpersonal and small group skills as important.

How does cooperative learning relate to the law?

Although not mentioned specifically in the law, cooperative learning is a support to carry out the law's requirement to provide students with needed supplementary aids and services. It does so by enabling them to make progress toward annual goals, be involved in and make progress in the general curriculum, and be educated and participate with nondisabled students.

Cooperative learning, inclusion, and broader school reform are part of an integral whole.

Cooperative learning is good for all students and . . . it is a part of comprehensive school reform efforts. To achieve this reform, teachers must work together to build networks within their school community. Teachers must also establish a cooperative classroom ethic that emphasizes overall community building, open communication about differences and classroom practices, and reciprocal helping relationships. Meaningful content in cooperative lessons is critical for the success of all students. For students to succeed within their groups, careful consideration regarding group heterogeneity must be given in conjunction with roles that ensure active, equal participation by all students. Creative assessment practices must be developed to document achievement of meaningful outcomes for students. All these considerations require planning and structure in order for the teaching to be successful.[40]

What are "best practices" of cooperative learning?

There are a number of cooperative learning "systems." A review of the literature on this topic in the *Harvard Education Letter* (May/June 2000) indicates that the various systems differ in the following ways: the amount of structure provided; the kinds of rewards offered; the methods used to hold students individually accountable; and the use of group competition. Among the major systems the *Harvard Education Letter* identifies are the following:

Student Learning Team (SLT): Developed initially by Bob Slavin at Johns Hopkins University, the emphasis in SLT is on team goals and team success. There are several SLT programs, some used across different grades and subjects, while others are specific to math (grades 3–6) and reading and writing (grades 3–5).

Learning Together: Developed at the University of Minnesota by David Johnson and Roger Johnson. Four or five-member heterogeneous groups work together on a common assignment. A single product is produced and the group receives a reward together. Emphasis is on team-building activities and how well the group works together.

Jigsaw: Developed initially as a way to replace competition with cooperation in the classroom, students are divided into "jigsaw groups," each with five or six members, diverse in terms of gender, ethnicity, race, and ability. Each member is given a segment of the assigned material to study. Once familiar with the material, members of each group who had the same assigned segment regroup in an "expert group," where they discuss the assigned material and prepare for their presentation to the "jigsaw group." Members return to their "jigsaw group" and each presents/teaches a segment to the whole group. Members are encouraged to ask questions for understanding and the teacher rotates among the groups. The unit is completed with a quiz on the material.

Kagan Structures: An eclectic approach that addresses the achievement of standards for all in heterogenous classrooms using cooperative learning. Material is available covering English and Language Arts, Mathematics, Science, and Social Studies, with particular adaptations for students with disabilities and English as Second Language Learners. A number of cooperative learning strategies have been developed by Kagan. They appear below.

Cooperative learning strategies[41]

Round robin: Each student shares something with classmates.

Corners: Teacher presents four alternatives; students divide into four groups and move to corners of the room. Students discuss and then listen to and paraphrase ideas from other groups.

Pairs check: Students work in pairs within groups of four. In pairs, students alternate as one solves a problem while the other coaches. After every two problems, one pair checks to see if they have the same answer as the other pair.

Think-pair share: Students think to themselves about a teacher provided topic; they then pair up with another student to discuss it, and then share their thoughts with the whole class.

Team word-webbing: Students write simultaneously on a piece of chart paper; drawing main concepts and supporting elements and bridges.

Co-op: Students work in groups to produce a group product to share with the whole class; each student makes a contribution to the group.

Jigsaw: Each student becomes an expert on one topic by working with members from other teams that are assigned the corresponding topic. Upon returning to the team, each one in turn teaches the group on the expert topic. All students are assessed on all aspects of the topic.

What is peer support?

In many ways, cooperative learning is a form of peer support. Peer support programs also can have a social interaction focus as well as an instructional one (e.g., peer-mediated instruction[42]). Among the socially-focused programs are buddy programs, pal groups, and Circle of Friends. While sometimes called "natural supports," they are intentional efforts to expand the social network of students with disabilities. Experience in many schools is that such activities become the basis for ongoing relationships among students, both in school and in the community.

What are "best practices" of peer support?

Among instructionally-based peer programs are peer initiated training, peer monitoring, and peer tutoring. Some peer tutoring programs involve nondisabled students tutoring students with disabilities. Student tutors expand the resource of those providing instruction, as well as offer opportunities for disabled and nondisabled students to work together. Utley (2001) says that peer –mediated instruction addresses the important class room question of differentiating instruction. She asserts that peer-mediated instruction and interventions;

> may serve as an effective strategy that (a) facilitates the inclusion of students with disabilities into general education classroom settings, (b) enhances academic achievement on standardized tests and curriculum-specific measures, (c) improves inter-personal relationships and the acceptance of individual differences among diverse students, and (d) improves student discipline in a proactive and positive manner.[43]

Maheady et al. (2001) summarize two earlier literature reviews[44] of peer mediated instruction and intervention (PMII), particularly for students with mild disabilities. The 1991 review reported that PMII produced noticeable pupil improvements in three distinct yet interrelated domains, i.e., academic, interpersonal, personal/social development.

[P]eer-teaching systems worked because they created more learner-friendly instructional environments. That is, they established more favorable pupil-teacher ratios within the classroom, increased student on-task time and response opportunities, provided additional opportunities for pupils to receive positive and corrective feedback, and enhanced pupils' opportunities to receive individualized help and encouragement. Moreover, students have consistently preferred peer-teaching practices over more traditional instructional arrangements (i.e., teacher-led and student-regulated activities).[45]

The 1997 survey, after confirming the positive effects that PMII has on pupils' basic academic skills, reported that:

> PMII components are highly effective for students with special needs because they allow teachers to individualize instruction on a classwide basis, and the academic and social benefits associated with such programs can be extended to nondisabled pupils in the same settings. Utley et al. suggested further that PMII may also provide an effective and efficient method for minimizing the excessive workloads that presently confront general education teachers. For example, peer monitoring procedures may assist in the correction and feedback process; peer modeling, tutoring, and group-oriented contingencies may facilitate the development of pupil's social skills without additional time allocations; and positive social networks might greatly enhance the general classroom climate in many schools.[46]

Bringing the findings up-to-date, Maheady et al. (2001) report on a Class-Wide Peer-Assisted Self-Management (CWPASM) program that improved student behaviors and class climate; ClassWide Peer Tutoring (CWPT) that showed powerful academic effects in second language acquisition and literacy[47]; Peer-Assisted Learning Strategies (PALS) that addressed literacy and mathematics instruction to facilitate the successful inclusion of students with mild disabilities in general education settings[48]; Classwide Student Tutoring Teams (CSTT) which produced substantial academic gains (e.g., all students with disabilities obtained passing grades) in the mathematics performance of students with mild disabilities enrolled in general education settings.[49]

Additional power is gained when disabled students are offered the opportunity themselves to be tutors. A recent meta-analysis provides support for designs that involve students with disabilities as tutors.[50] This may take the form of a cross-age model, where older students with a disability tutor younger children without a disability. Here, the student with a disability gains the benefit of learning through teaching. Factors contributing to the power of such a design include: the status of being recognized as someone who is able to give (not always receive) help and take responsibility, and, as such, being viewed as someone who is capable of achievement and worthy of respect.[51] Additionally this design provides the opportunity to review material as one prepares to tutor and to focus on learning as the tutor seeks to connect with the tutee.[52] Students with any disability can assume the tutor role. An interesting design has been developed in New Orleans where older students with emotional disturbance/behavior disorders serve as mentors to younger at-risk proteges.[53]

When all students have a chance to play the role of both tutor and tutee, a pro-learning atmosphere, one which is cooperative and collegial, is more likely to develop in the classroom. Collaborative designs reject deficit-based education models, that promote segregated dual systems. Instead, they provide the basis for restructuring education systems to develop programs that serve all students together, and serve them well.

Drawing from the theoretical work of Jean Piaget, Lev Vygotsky, and Harry Stack; Damon (1984) summarizes the case for all students being involved.

Because peer tutoring is of demonstrable value both to tutor and tutee, an ideal school approach would expose children to both roles. Any child has an area of competence that can be imparted to a younger or less sophisticated child. Conversely, all children can benefit from tutoring in areas in which they are relative novices. In assuming both tutor and tutee roles, children not only gain the benefits of tutee as well as tutor, but also a highly informative experience in role reversal. The child's switching from expert to novice can impart to the child deeper and more sympathetic understanding of the educational endeavor.[54]

While peer programs often develop on an informal basis, those that are most effective are planned and structured. In some school districts, which have community service requirements, peer support activities are incorporated. Training of tutors is a valuable component of peer support programs. A junior high school peer buddies program in West Feliciana Parish, LA, includes disability awareness as part of the training, as it sets clear guidelines for the buddies (e.g., don't talk down to the student, don't provide help without being asked, don't coddle the student with a disability, don't treat her/him like a child). A Virginia peer program emphasizes the importance of praise that is specific to performance, including reinforcement for successful performance.

The benefits for the "tutor" can be both cognitive and affective. In the cognitive domain, a review in the *Harvard Education Letter* reported that "[t]utors learn at least as much as the students they teach—and tutors who are far behind academically gain even more."[55] For the tutors, tutoring offers the opportunity to practice activities in which learning has occurred but mastery has not yet been achieved or those in which learning is not yet generalized to other settings. Tutors learn by reviewing, reinforcing, reformulating the material from another setting, as well as learning from a different vantage point. First characterized as "learning through teaching" in programs developed in the 1960s,[56] the idea of involving students with disabilities in the tutor role was introduced in the 1970s.[57] One of the first of these programs was conducted in Central Harlem by the New Careers Training Laboratory, then at Queens College, The City University of New York. Both tutors and tutees gained academic, behavioral, and social skills. A decade later, Brigham Young University conducted a three-year project, "Handicapped Children as Tutors." Students with mental retardation and those with learning disabilities tutored both similarly disabled and nondisabled students. Research findings on the project found that:

- Handicapped children functioned effectively as tutors. They can learn to demonstrate instructional content, monitor tutee performance, and give appropriate feedback.
- Both tutors and tutees experienced growth in the topic tutored.
- Parents, teachers, and tutees perceived reverse-role tutoring as an effective intervention strategy in special education.[58]

The following is a report from an 11th grade non-disabled student who served as a peer assistant, teaching students about weight lifting as part of meeting a service requirement in a Howard County (MD) school. It illustrates the affective benefits for the nondisabled tutor.

It's difficult for me to express what I have learned because working with significantly impaired special education students has changed me and changed my life for the better in a way that I can't communicate. When I signed up for this class, I took it because I needed an easy elective to pull up my GPA. I never guessed that I would end up working so much and so hard. I never guessed I could care so deeply about anyone or anything.

Before I became an aide, I came to school late every day. This is because I was so focused on being at every party, drinking as much as I could and cruising around in my car faster than I should whenever possible. That was my life. I didn't care about school. Now, I have people who need me. I've had to change my life style. I want to go to college and major in special education now. Before, my parents wanted me to go to college but I didn't care. I really didn't think I was good enough to make it in college either. I have discovered that I can really make a difference in the lives of these kids. I felt a responsibility to be a better person, to work harder and to learn more.

I know a lot of teachers think guys like me don't deserve to be an aide. They think it should be a job reserved for GT [Gifted & Talented] people. I guess they don't believe all that stuff they preach about seeing people as a glass half filled instead of half empty. I'm starting to believe that stuff too. About the intensity five students, and even about myself.

I have also discovered that I have guts I didn't know I had. When the guys use the word 'retard' as an insult, I know now that it's a disability, not an insult. I feel so sick when they say that I can't just play along with the gag anymore. I have to speak up now. I've become an advocate. I am not sure how this happened to me; it wasn't something I ever thought I could do.

[I] think having these students in regular classes has made our school a better place. I think it has made people think. One day a bunch of us guys were talking about what it would be like to have kids of our own. We all had our TV sitcom ideas about what it would be like. And when we thought about what it would be like if our kid was born with mental retardation. That was really heavy stuff to talk about! Maybe its normal for the smart honor student types to sit around and worry about real life but for me and my dumb jock-type friends to get that serious is scary! This school is really different since intensity five came to town. It made everybody have to become better people than we were before the program.[59]

What are the roles of administrators regarding cooperative learning and peer mediated learning?

Both cooperative learning and peer mediated learning are activities that can take place within a single teacher's classroom; as such, they need no special administrative arrangements. Opportunities for professional development may be necessary, especially to familiarize teachers with the various cooperative learning and peer mediated designs. A significant aspect of the training is the role change for teachers, from being the sole dispenser of knowledge to organizing and facilitating students as active providers of knowledge to their peers.

When cooperative learning and peer mediated learning activities are a common feature of the general education classroom, the IEP Team can rely upon them as a "natural" support for a student with disabilities. Otherwise, their use may be incorporated as a specific supplementary aid in the student's IEP. Should this be a strategy with which the general education teacher is not familiar, professional development for the teacher can be incorporated in the student's IEP.

Well-designed and carefully implemented, cooperative learning and peer mediated learning may dissipate parental and teacher concerns as to the twin pitfalls of failing to engage the student for whom the material is quickly understood or the student who needs more time or greater depth. Cooperative learning lessons where everyone performs the same activity fail to tap the richness of the strategy. Tasks can be differentiated by quantity as well as complexity, so as to appropriately engage all learners.

An example of such a lesson:

> In a "jigsaw" activity, designed for heterogeneous groups of four or five, each student reads a segment of a succinct biography of Harriet Tubman. Students with special needs review a relatively short segment of the book with a resource teacher before the class assignment. Students able to comprehend more complex material read a more demanding section of the book. Other students receive portions that appropriately challenge them. Students summarize their reading, report to one another, review their findings together, and are responsible for knowing information about all aspects of Tubman's life. Students demonstrate their knowledge by answering the teacher's questions, completing a group project, taking a quiz, or performing a skit. Each person's contribution, no matter its complexity, is essential for the group to be successful.[60]

Similarly, as discussed above, well-designed and conducted peer mediated learning programs benefit both tutor and tutee. This is especially the case when students have the opportunity to play both roles.

Where can I find additional information about cooperative learning? Peer mediated learning?

For information about specific cooperative learning "systems," the following are available:

Student Team Learning developed by Robert Slavin and colleagues at Johns Hopkins University, Center for Research on the Education of Students Placed at Risk. www.csos.jhu.edu.

Learning Together developed by David Johnson and Robert Johnson, Cooperative Learning Center, University of Minnesota. *www.clerc.com.*

Jigsaw developed initially by Elliot Aronson and colleagues at the University of California, Santa Cruz, and subsequently modified at Johns Hopkins. *elliott@cats.ucsc.edu.*

Kagan Structures developed by Spencer, Miguel and Laurie Kagan, *www.KaganOnline.com.* S. Kagan, M. Kagan, & L. Kagan (2000). *Reaching standards through cooperative learning: Providing for ALL learners in general education classrooms* (I. English/Language Arts, II. Science, III. Mathematics, IV. Social Studies). Port Chester, NY: National Professional Resources, Inc. This is a four volume handbook applying cooperative learning for diverse learners.

Putting cooperative learning to the test, (May/June 2000), *Harvard Education Letter*, 16(3), 1–6.

7

Positive Behavior Supports

Just for the fun of it: Test yourself on your current knowledge of positive behavior supports

For which students are positive behavior supports important?

_____

_____

Turn to page 102 to read about this topic.

How does classroom instruction affect student (mis)behavior?

_____

_____

Turn to page 104 to read about this topic.

What is the relationship between overall school policies, classroom practices, and individual student (mis)behavior?

_____

_____

Turn to page 106 to read about this topic.

What are the factors that lead to student misbehavior? How can they be countered?

_____

_____

Turn to page 107 to read about this topic.

How can the climate of a classroom be measured?

_____

_____

Turn to page 108 to read about this topic.

What are positive behavior supports?

Positive behavior supports describe the overall efforts of schools to provide a safe and orderly learning environment for all students. This ensures that students with disabilities receive the free appropriate public education (FAPE) to which they are entitled, per IDEA; it also ensures that their nondisabled peers receive the education to which they are entitled.

How do positive behavior supports relate to the law?

Attention to individual student behavior has always been a concern in special education law, primarily in the development of services for students with severe emotional disturbance (SED). In recent years, as violence has become an issue for the nation's schools,[61] Congress has addressed behavior issues in various pieces of legislation. One of these is in the reauthorized IDEA; therein behavior is identified as one of the special factors that the IEP Team must consider. If a child's behavior interferes with her/his learning or the learning of others, the IEP Team, using a Functional Assessment of Behavior (FAB), must consider strategies and supports to address that behavior and, as appropriate, incorporate them in the IEP in the form of a Behavioral Intervention Plan (BIP).

When and for whom are positive behavior supports needed?

The goal of providing a safe learning environment requires positive behavior supports be in place for all students. There has been a charge that the provisions of IDEA hinder school discipline by allowing students with disabilities to use negative behavior that would not be tolerated from nondisabled students. Also, that students with disabilities are not allowed to be punished for the same misbehavior that would lead to punishment for nondisabled students. The thinking of advocates, reflected in IDEA regulations, is that if the misbehavior is a function of the student's disability, then the appropriate response is to change the student's program not punish him or her. In response to such concerns, Congress commissioned a study, conducted by its investigative arm, the U.S. General Accounting Office in 2001. The overall findings of the study were that, "students with disabilities who are involved in violence or other serious incidents at school are being punished in the same way as other students who commit comparable acts . . . ."[62] The study, based on a survey of middle and high school principals, reported that both students with and without disabilities received suspensions of a similar length, and that both groups were expelled from school or placed in alternative settings at about the same rate, e.g., about one in six of those who engaged in serious misconduct. Principals generally rated their schools special-education-discipline policies, both those under IDEA and local policies, as having a positive or neutral effect on school safety and orderliness.[63] On the other hand, about a fifth of the principals objected to a separate discipline policy for students with disabilities and found the IDEA procedures burdensome and time-consuming.

There is increasing attention in education to addressing the behavioral barriers to learning present in schools, identifying the schools' role in fostering negative behaviors as well as their role in encouraging and supporting students' positive behavior. Among the myriad of terms used are discipline programs, violence prevention, behavior management, and classroom management. In this book, misbehavior will be used to denote the behavior being addressed and positive behavior support will be used to describe the intervention.

Before turning to the approaches used in positive behavior support programs there are some basic factors to keep in mind:

- The IDEA presumption of serving students in the general education environment with the necessary supplementary aids and services.

- The IDEA requirement that schools address the full range of the student's educational needs, social and emotional, as well as academic; just as the student's disability may entail academic consequences requiring special education services to provide FAPE, so, too, the disability may entail social and behavioral consequences requiring special education services to provide FAPE.

- The provisions of IDEA and the obligations of school districts to meet the needs of individual students with disabilities, require a coordinated approach among the home environment, the school, and the classroom.

- An overall consistent school approach requires successful classroom practices such as:

- effective engagement of the student in the learning activities,

- focus on the activities of both the child and the teacher,

- serve to defuse the immediate issue(s),

- prevent its extension,

- develop alternative behaviors, and

- address the consequences for the other students in the class.[64]

There are numerous issues to consider in regard to the assessment of student behavior. The interdisciplinary nature of the IEP Team provides the forum for such consideration and for determining the nature and location of needed services. Some national data provide context for local considerations:

- Greater than half of the referrals for special education are based on emotional or behavioral issues that occur when the student is in grades 3 through 6.

- Almost three-fourths of such referrals are boys.

- The most common factor identified in these referrals for both boys and girls is poor peer relationships; others include frustration, low achievement, withdrawn behaviors, disruptive behavior, fighting, refusal to work, and short attention span.

- A disproportionate percentage of Black students are referred for emotional or behavioral issues, are certified with such labels, and are placed in more restrictive settings.

What are the "best practices" of positive behavior support?

In developing a positive behavior support program for individual students, there are a number of factors that are enablers of success and others that may be seen as inhibitors.

Enablers

- A sense of urgency usually surrounds events of serious student misbehavior.

- There is a growing body of successful experience that can be called upon.

- A child-centered focus leads to measurable outcomes.

- Educators can relate to the pedagogic approach of positive behavior support.

- Changes in IDEA promote positive behavior support efforts.

* The failure of punishment and exclusion has been well documented

- The process provides opportunities for educators and families to collaborate.

- A well-developed support plan can have far-reaching positive outcomes for child, family, and school.

Inhibitors

- The initial point of entry is often in response to crisis.

- The process takes time and may involve a reassignment of resources.

- Often schools are seeking a quick fix.

- Positive behavior support requires a team approach and ongoing commitment from school personnel.

- The exigencies of school life too often preclude the needed follow through

Underlying all positive behavior support systems are a set of four assumptions:

1. *Challenging behaviors are context related.* They occur for a reason and are not simply a manifestation of the individual's disability. When they do occur they likely signal that something in the prevailing environment is disturbing or provoking the individual.

2. *Challenging behaviors serve a function for the student.* While socially unacceptable, these behaviors enable the student to escape or avoid unpleasant events, gain access to desired activities or social interactions.

3. *Effective interventions are based on a thorough understanding of the person, his or her social contexts, and the function of the problem behavior.*

4. *Positive behavior support must be grounded in person-centered values that respect the dignity, preferences, and goals of each student.*[65]

Teachers have a key role in gathering information and managing student disruptive behavior. While not ignoring the consequences of the child's disability, it is important for the teacher first to address questions concerning the overall activities of the classroom.

Some examples are as follows:

- Is the instructional program appropriate to meet the student's needs?
- Are needed related services and supplementary aids and services in place?
- Is the student effectively engaged in the learning activities?
- Does the student understand the concepts being taught?
- Does the student have the study skills necessary to learn the material?
- Are there factors of physical arrangement, boredom or frustration that limit the student's learning?
- Does the student know the processes of transition? From one activity to another? From one setting to another?

Extra-school factors, such as issues in the student's home or family life must be considered.

In gathering information about the student and circumstances that surround the misbehavior, the following questions may serve as a guide:

- When is the student most likely to engage in problem behaviors?
- What specific events appear to be contributing to the problem situation?
- What function(s) does the problem behavior serve for the student?
- What might the student be communicating?
- When is the student less likely to engage in problem behaviors?

After collecting information about the nature and setting of a student's misbehavior, the function and the possible intent of the behavior(s) can be considered. With an understanding of the intent of the problem behavior(s), appropriate strategies can then be developed. The following table of "Misbehavior Messages" may serve as a guide in understanding the function and the possible meaning of the misbehavior. The next table provides a guide of "Proactive Strategies" to preclude misbehavior.

Misbehavior Messages

Function	Possible messages
To gain access to social interaction	"Play with me."
	"Watch what I am doing."
	"Did I do good work?"
	"Spend time with me."
	"Let's do this together."
	"Can I have a turn, too?"
	"I want to be one of the group."
To gain access to activities, objects.	"I want to play outside."
	"Can I have what s/he has?"
	"I don't want to stop this."
	"I'm hungry."
To terminate/avoid unwanted situations	"Leave me alone."
	"This is too hard."
	"I need help."
	"I don't want to do this."
	"Don't tell me what to do."
	"I don't like to be teased."
	"I'm bored."
	"I'm not feeling well."
	"I need a break."
To gain access to stimulating events	" I like doing this."[66]

Schoolwide positive behavior support systems

In recent years, student discipline programs have shifted from a sole focus on an individual student with a "problem" behavior to the need for school-wide behavior support systems. Instead of a patchwork of individual behavior management plans, schools are moving toward a systemic approach that addresses the classroom, areas outside of the classroom, and the individual student.

In building *school-wide systems*, the following approaches have been successful:

- a small number of clear behavioral expectations are defined,
- teaching of these behavioral expectations is the role of all staff,
- appropriate behaviors are acknowledged,
- behavioral errors are corrected systematically and proactively,
- administrative support and involvement are ongoing, and
- classroom and individual student support systems are integrated within the school-wide system.

Proactive strategies		
Strategy	*Instructional example*	*Social example*
Remove a problem event	Avoid giving difficult word problems for independent seatwork Avoid requiring repetitive tasks	Avoid crowded settings Avoid long delays
Modify a problem event	Shorten lessons Reduce the number of problems on a page Modify instruction to decrease errors Increase lesson pace	Change voice intonation Modify a boring schedule Use suggestive rather than directive language
Intersperse difficult or unpleasant events with easy or pleasant events	Mix difficult problems with easier ones Mix mastered tasks with acquisition Tasks for seatwork	Schedule nonpreferred activities with preferred ones Precede directives for non-preferred activities with easily followed directions
Add events that promote desired behaviors	Provide choice of tasks, materials, activities Include student preferences Use cooperative learning strategies to encourage participation State clear expectations at start of lesson	Schedule preferred activities in daily routines Provide a variety of activities Provide opportunities for social interactions Provide opportunities for physical movement
Block or neutralize the impact of negative events	Offer frequent breaks Reduce demands when student upset	Provide opportunities for rest Provide time alone Provide time to regroup after negative experience

"Unified discipline" is one among many systemwide programs. While particular to that program, the following features can be considered more generally.

Unified attitudes: All participants adopt a consistent point of view about encouraging appropriate behavior and correcting misbehavior. All participants support the belief that all students are able to improve their behavior. All participants provide correction in a professional manner and support the belief that anger and emotional upset undermine instructional effectiveness.

Unified expectations: All participants reach consensus on school rules, classroom rules, and classroom procedures. Unified sets of rules are developed across each grade.

Unified correction: A uniform verbal correction procedure and a consistent set of consequences is developed.

Unified team roles: Support is available for students who are difficult to manage, and clear roles and responsibilities are established for the entire school team.

Classroom positive behavior support systems

Classwide systems must be developed and implemented aligned with the school-wide system.

The following materials provide guiding questions:
- "Developing Classroom Expectations and Routines: A Self-Study Guide," Blackline Master No. 12, page 114.
- "Effective Classroom Management Practices: A Self-Study Guide," Blackline Master No. 13, page 115.
- "Approaches of School, Classroom, and Student-Focused Practices: A Self-Study Guide," Blackline Master No. 14, page 116.

Measuring the climate of a classroom—that hum of engaged work—is a subtle matter. The Pennsylvania instructional support system suggests four areas of attention at the classroom level and five areas in terms of individual students.

Classroom-based indicators of the need for change:
1. *Disruptive behavior.* As a general rule, a problem exists if disruptive behaviors occur more than once per hour (or class period) on the average.
2. *On-task rates.* Problematic if more than 2 or 3 students are off-task at any given time.
3. *Completion of assignments.* Generally a problem if 10 percent or more of the students often do not complete their work on time.
4. *Student cooperation.* A problem is if after a few weeks of school students continue to need constant reminders to follow classroom procedures.

Individual student indicators of the need for change:
1. *Lack of increases in alternative skills,*
2. *Lack of reduction in problem behaviors,*
3. *Lack of maintenance or generalization of alternative skills,*
4. *Limited lifestyle enhancements,*
5. *Student and/or family displeasure in impact/outcomes.*

What are the roles of administrators, clinicians, and parents regarding positive behavior supports?

Positive behavior supports for individual students must be embedded in a school-wide program of positive behavior support. The establishment of such a program and the commitment of the necessary resources and follow–through are central activities of school administration. Developing a school-wide plan involves the systematic collection of data and analysis, the development of a consensus-based body of behavioral expectations and consequences (positive and negative), establishment of a school policy (consonant with federal and state law and district policy), allocation of staff resources to develop and implement the system, and support for regular review and revision. Each of these features of a school-wide positive behavior support program will require administrative involvement and support.

When the classroom teacher has had support but can no longer effectively address the behavioral issues of a student independently, it may be appropriate to take additional steps. This begins when the IEP Team considers "behavior" issues and, as needed, the completion of a Functional Behavioral Assessment (FBA) and the development of a Behavior Intervention Plan (BIP). The presence of the classroom teacher as a member of the IEP Team supports grounding the FBA in the activities of the classroom. As the BIP is developed, clinicians may play a role in assisting classroom teachers in its implementation. Regardless of who is involved in the implementation, it is essential that the BIP be integral with the student's overall learning program, academic, behavioral, and social.

Parental involvement in developing a positive behavior support program for an individual student is essential. This includes involvement in the conduct of the Functional Behavioral Assessment, the development of the behavior intervention plan, the consideration of "antecedent" events, the development and reinforcement of alternative skills, and the establishment of lifestyle interventions. While home and school are different environments, each can support the other in promoting positive student behavior. Most parents are willing to be involved in creating positive behavior, and may request support in gaining new skills in this area. Indeed, such training is one of the most frequent requests from parents. In conducting such training, parent-to-parent activities are an important resource.

Administrative involvement and support are essential in a whole school approach to positive behavior. A message from the U.S. Department of Education provides a guide for administrators.

Prevention Research & the IDEA Discipline Provisions:
A Guide for School Administrators

The following was conveyed as an e-mail message to school superintendents by Judith E. Heumann, Assistant Secretary, Office of Special Education and Rehabilitative Services, and Kenneth Warlick, Director, Office of Special Education Programs, US Department of Education, January 2001.

An Ounce of Prevention

The Challenge: Creating, Safe, Effective, and Orderly Learning Environments
- To be effective learning environments, schools need to be safe and orderly.
- Problem behavior is the single most common reason why students are referred for removal from school.
- Challenges facing educators are significant and persistent.
- Across the nation schools are being asked to do more with less.
- Punishment and exclusion remain the most common responses to problem behavior by students.
- Reprimands, detention, and exclusion are documented as *ineffective* strategies for improving the behavior of students.

Impact of the Challenge: How Negative Behavior Impacts Schools
- Loss of instructional time for all students
- Exclusion of students
- Time away from teaching and learning
- Overemphasis on reactive discipline & classroom management practices to control behavior
- Chaotic school environments that disenfranchise families & school staff
- Ineffective & inefficient use of student and staff resources & time

A Systematic Solution: Creating School Wide Responses
- Creating of host environments that support preferred & effective practices, and include:
- policies (proactive discipline handbooks, procedural handbooks)
- structures (behavior support teams)
- routines (opportunities for students to learn expected behavior, staff development, data-based decision-making)
- Schools successful in dealing with behavior realize that all children need behavior support. They define, teach, monitor, and acknowledge appropriate social behavior for all students. They do not wait for students to fail before providing behavior supports.
- Establishment of proactive environments that have the capacity to identify, adapt, and sustain effective policies, systems, and research validated practices.
- Focus attention on creating and sustaining school environments that improve results for all children by making problem behavior less effective, efficient, and relevant; and desired behavior more functional.

Continuum of Effective Behavior Support

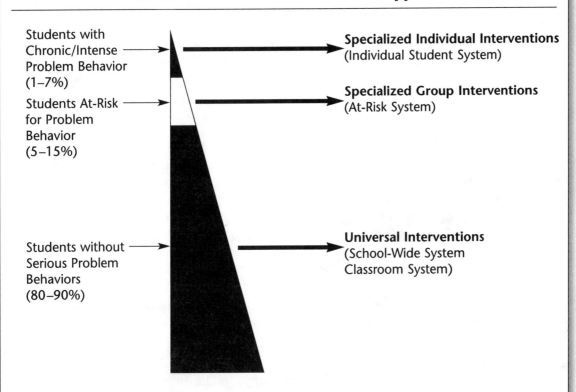

Students with Chronic/Intense Problem Behavior (1–7%) → **Specialized Individual Interventions** (Individual Student System)

Students At-Risk for Problem Behavior (5–15%) → **Specialized Group Interventions** (At-Risk System)

Students without Serious Problem Behaviors (80–90%) → **Universal Interventions** (School-Wide System Classroom System)

Positive Behavioral Intervention and Supports: A Brief Summary

- Positive behavior support is the application of positive behavioral interventions & systems to achieve positive change.

- Positive behavior support is an approach to discipline & intervention that is proving effective and practical in schools.

- Positive behavior change is the application of the science of behavior to achieve socially important change. The emphasis is on behavior change that is durable, comprehensive, and linked to academic & social gains.

- As a general matter, positive behavior support should be applied before any child is excluded from school due to a problem behavior.

- The development of positive behavioral interventions & plans that are guided by functional behavioral assessment (FBA) is a foundation on which positive behavioral support is delivered.

- Functional behavioral assessment (FBA) is a systematic way of identifying problem behaviors and the events that predict occurrence, non-occurrence, and maintenance of those behaviors.

- Strong, administrative leadership, support & participation is needed for effective efforts.

- Positive behavior support considers multiple contexts, including community, family, district, school, classroom, non-classroom, and individual.

- A proactive perspective is maintained along a continuum, using primary (what we do for all), secondary (what we do for some), and tertiary (what we do for a few) prevention & interventions.

Data Supported Evidence

- Schools implementing systemic strategies of problem behavior prevention report reductions in office discipline referrals of 20–60%.

- Schools implementing systemic strategies of problem behavior prevention report improved access to academic engaged time & improved academic performance.

- The success rate for interventions based on a prior functional assessment is almost twice that obtained when this type of assessment is not conducted.

Legal Requirements Under the Law

In the IDEA amendments of 1997, Congress recognized that in certain instances, school personnel needed increased flexibility to deal with safety issues while maintaining the needed due process protections in the IDEA.

What the law allows:

- School personnel can remove a student with a disability, for 10 consecutive schools days or less, at a time for a violation of the school code of conduct (to the same extent applied to children without disabilities). School personnel can immediately remove, for up to 10 consecutive school days or less, the same child for separate instances of misconduct.

- School personnel can also order a change of placement of a child with a disability to an appropriate interim alternative educational setting, for up to 45 days, for possession of weapons or drugs or the solicitation or sale of controlled substances while at school and school functions.

- If school personnel believe that a child is dangerous to him- or herself or others, they can ask a hearing officer in an expedited due process hearing to remove a student to an interim alternative educational setting for up to 45 days.

- 45 day interim alternative educational placements can be extended in additional 45-day increments if the hearing officer agrees that the child continues to be substantially likely to injure him- or herself or others if returned to his or her prior placement.

- School personnel can remove a child with a disability, including suspending or expelling for behavior that is not a manifestation of the child's disability, to the same extent as is done for children without disabilities, for the same behavior.

- School personnel can report crimes to appropriate law enforcement and judicial authorities.

- School personnel can always ask a court for a temporary restraining order in order to protect children or adults from harmful behaviors.

Where can I find additional information about positive behavior supports?

Overall information is available from The Center on Positive Behavioral Intervention and Supports, 5262 University of Oregon, Eugene, OR 97403–5262, (541) 346–2505. Their Web Site is at *www.pbis.org*. Information on school safety and violence prevention is available from the Center for Effective Collaboration and Practice, 1000 Thomas Jefferson Street, NW, Washington, DC 20007 (888) 457–1551. Their Web Site is at www.air.org/cecp.

In the past several years, many state education departments have developed material in this area.

Notable has been the work in Pennsylvania and Michigan. See esp.,

T. Knoster (N.D.). *Tips for educators: Behavior support. . . . Effective schools.* Harrisburg, PA: Instructional Support Systems of Pennsylvania.

L.M. Bambara & T. Knoster (1998). *Designing positive behavior support plans.* Washington, DC. American Association on Mental Retardation.

Positive Behavior Support for ALL Michigan Students (September 6, 2000). Lansing, MI: State Board of Education.

A number of schoolwide and/or classroom programs have been developed in the past several years. Most include materials and training services. Some of the well-recognized programs include:

Effective Behavior Support (EBS) Program. Tim Lewis, Department of Special Education, University of Missouri, 313 Townsend Hall, Columbia, MO 65211.

The Beacons of Excellence. Doug Chaney, Department of Special Education, University of Washington, PO Box 353600, Seattle, WA 98195.

Unified Discipline. Richard White, College of Education, University of North Carolina, Charlotte, NC 28223.

PAR (Preventing, Acting upon, and Resolving troubling behaviors). Michael Rosenberg, Department of Special Education, Johns Hopkins University, 100 Whitehead Hall, Baltimore, MD 21218.

Project Achieve. Howard Knoff, School Psychology Program, University of South Florida, 4202 East Fowler Avenue, Tampa, FL 33620.

Bullyproof Programs. Center for Research on Women, Wellesley College, Wellesley, MA 02481.

Positive Behavior Support. Tim Knoster, Interagency Support Project, CSIU, PO Box 213, Lewisburg, PA 17837.

Behavioral and Educational Strategies for Teachers (BEST). Utah's Project BEST, State Office of Education, 250 East 500 South, Salt Lake City, UT 8411.

Montana Behavior Intervention (MBI). Office of Public Instruction, PO Box 202501, Helena, MT 59620.

Cooperative Discipline. Cooperative Discipline Foundation, 1020 Westbrooke Lane, Easly, SC 29642.

DEVELOPING CLASSROOM EXPECTATIONS AND ROUTINES: A SELF-STUDY GUIDE

Effective instructional activities can engage students, and, as a consequence, make misbehavior less likely.

• Am I teaching useful, appropriate, and important knowledge and skills to the students?

_____

_____

• Am I using effective instructional strategies and curricula to teach these skills and knowledge?

_____

_____

• Have I taught classroom rules and expectations directly to the students?

_____

_____

• Have students demonstrated mastery of classroom expectations and routines?

_____

_____

• What obstacles prevent students from performing desired classroom expectations and routines?

_____

_____

• Have I taught and do I use procedures for encouraging appropriate displays of classroom rules and expectations?

_____

_____

• Have I taught and do I use a continuum of procedures for discouraging/preventing rule violation?

_____

_____

• Do I modify my instruction to maximize student learning and to accommodate individual student differences?

_____

_____

• Do I have procedures in place for monitoring student behavior and the effectiveness of my classroom management practices?

_____

_____

Inclusion: A Service, Not A Place, by Alan Gartner and Dorothy Kerzner Lipsky

EFFECTIVE CLASSROOM MANAGEMENT PRACTICES: A SELF-STUDY GUIDE

While not every classroom problem can be anticipated, there is empirical evidence of effective classroom practices. Teachers using such practices can often preclude problems. The following questions can serve as a guide.

- Do I provide advance organizers or pre-corrections?

These function as reminders of expected behaviors before students enter into a situation where problem behaviors many be manifested. For example, before students are to move to the next activity, the teacher says," Be sure you collect all your materials, put your completed papers on my desk, and line up."

- Are students kept engaged?

To engage students, the instructional activity must maintain their attention, positive reinforcement provided, and access to positive reinforcement for other activities minimized.

- Is a positive focus provided?

The activity must be presented in a positive light, more positive than negative interactions provided, problem behaviors anticipated and cut short.

- Are classroom rules consistently enforced?

Rules for all students must be consistent.

- Are rule violations and social behavior errors corrected pro-actively?

In the context of a previously established rule, error correction should be routine and not divert from the lesson itself.

- Do I plan smooth transitions?

It is important to alert students to the transition, inform them of the expected behavior, follow routines consistently, and provide regular feedback to students.

Inclusion: A Service, Not A Place, by Alan Gartner and Dorothy Kerzner Lipsky.

APPROACHES OF SCHOOL, CLASSROOM, AND STUDENT-FOCUSED PRACTICES: A SELF-STUDY GUIDE

When (mis)behavior by a student requires attention, there is a combination of school-wide policy, classroom procedures, and individual attention that must be considered. The following approaches can help a teacher to manage or forestall (mis)behavior. The approaches can serve as guiding questions for teachers to consider in their classroom practices.

In my classroom, do I:

- apply schoolwide rules,

_____

- explicitly teach schoolwide and class rules expectations/rules,

_____

- model and have students role play "problem" situations,

_____

- teach social skills and skills of self-management,

_____

- support students' setting personal goals,

_____

- teach students self-monitoring goals and encourage their use,

_____

- use positive correction prompts,

_____

- establish a clear set of consequences, positive and negative, for (mis)behavior,

_____

- build opportunities for movement within a lesson,

_____

- provide a structure ("scaffold") for the learning activity,

_____

- establish alternative work areas,

_____

- proactively decrease distractions and reduce unstructured activities,

_____

- provide active learning opportunities for student participation,

_____

- provide reminders/cues for appropriate behavior, and

_____

- explain the purposes and expectations for each activity?

_____

Inclusion: A Service, Not A Place, by Alan Gartner and Dorothy Kerzner Lipsky.

8

Technology,
Including Assistive Technology

Just for the fun of it: Test yourself on your current knowledge of assistive technology

How is technology used in schools? How does it differ from assistive technology?

_____

_____

Turn to page 118 to read about this topic.

For which students should technology be considered? Assistive technology?

_____

_____

Turn to page 119 to read about this topic.

How can technology be used to promote quality education for all students?

_____

_____

Turn to page 120 to read about this topic.

What are the questions to ask about regarding the use of technology?

_____

_____

Turn to page 122 to read about this topic.

How can technology be used as a tool for inclusion?

_____

_____

Turn to page 122 to read about this topic.

What is technology? Assistive technology? How are they used in the schools?

Technology in schools covers a wide gamut of devices and techniques, from a special grip on a pencil to a machine that provides oral presentation of print text, from simple devices to highly sophisticated systems. Greater demands in learning activities, as well as concerns that students be well equipped to enter the workforce, have led to an extraordinary expansion in the use of technology, especially computers, both for nondisabled students and for those with disabilities.[70] As of 1999, however, only 20 percent of the teachers in the nation's schools felt "well prepared" to use technology to support the curriculum and their teaching.[71]

Broadly, "assistive technology" refers to a range of technological tools and services designed to enable a student with disabilities to participate in schooling and to access the curriculum. They enable the user to be more self-confident, independent and more fully integrated into the classroom. Assistive technology is defined in the law as "any item, piece of equipment, or product system . . . that is used to increase, maintain, or improve functional capabilities of children with disabilities." While historically it has been considered for students with significant disabilities, increasingly various forms of assistive technology have been used with a wider range of students. Lee and Shireley (2000) identify the issue as too often schools talk about "technology in general education and assistive technology in special education." Instead, they propose that "we need to talk about technology in schools." Such comprehensive planning , they assert, is "more likely to result in cost effective purchases, increased staff collaboration, resource sharing and successful outcomes for all students within the system."[72] A tool that promotes embedding assistive technology in the broader frame of technology within the school is *Technology for all: A guide to solving the puzzle*.[73]

An extensive study by the David and Lucille Packard Foundation[74] reports that at home students 6 to 11 years of age averaged 27 minutes a day at the computer, while those 12 to 17 years of age averaged 63 minutes a day. Not only does the use of computers vary by the age of the child, it varies by access, what has been called the "digital divide."

There is variation as well in how schools use computers. Schools serving poor children are more likely to emphasize word processing and other simple tasks, while those serving a more affluent population more frequently use computers to promote problem solving and a deeper understanding of an area of study. Also, there is a gender gap in the use of computers. A report from the American Association of University Women Educational Foundation points to girls' reservations about the computer culture, as well as concerns regarding current ways girls participate in the computer culture.[75]

As would be expected, the absence of computers, greater in low income than higher income communities, is a barrier to the use of technology. But availability itself is not enough to address the issue of technology equity.[76] According to a report by the National Center on Educational Statistics, there are many barriers to the use of technology. These include: the absence of computers in classrooms and for student use at home, the lack of release time for teachers to learn how to use the computers, the lack of time in the schedule for computer use, the absence of good instructional software, the lack of support regarding ways to integrate technology into the curriculum, and outdated computers.[77] A report commissioned by the Software and Information Industry Association found that teacher professional development and decisions about how computers are to be used in instruction may matter more than how often technology is used.[78]

The Packard Foundation report points out that computers can be an especially effective learning tool for students with disabilities, both in providing physical access and improving spatial skills and visual attention. Teachers in the NCERI national study reported technology as an important instructional tool. In addition to the barrier represented by the limits of teacher training programs, the effective use of technology in the classroom for students with disabilities is limited by the lack of administrative support and demand for its use, the cost of (some) technology, and the policies of (some) school districts that limit the use of district-funded technology outside of the school, thus making it difficulty (if not impossible) for technology-dependent students to participate in educational and social activities after school.

In addition to the computer, which is clearly the most commonly used technology, there are many simple low-tech, less expensive solutions that can be used to assist students. These can be related to positioning, environmental control, mobility, self-care and even recreation. As technology's goal is to compensate for a deficit, its' uses are limited only by creativity and integrity!

While classroom practices overall need to respond to the increasing diversity of the nation's classrooms,[79] there are a number of web sites that provide access to quality literature that will introduce children to other cultural contexts.[80]

Technology as a "diversity accommodation tool," a concept developed by Pressman and Blackstone, challenges many of the assumptions about the use of technology and students with disabilities. These include the basic assumption about "readiness," as well assumptions such as: drill and practice with a computer reflects the "best practice" or is even a particularly effective way of mastering skills; standardized tests should be used in non-standardized ways with the kinds of students who were not originally used in the standardization pool; and that computer labs are an effective place to put computers to facilitate student learning.

With the increasing diversity of American classrooms, which more than ever are shared by children with various physical abilities, learning needs, and cultural backgrounds, schools need to understand technology tools as diversity accommodation tools. Many children with disabilities learn differently. Some simply learn more slowly. Many require adaptations and supports to access the curriculum. Computers are powerful tools that can provide multisensory information in ways that captivate and motivate students involved in the learning process.

Computer use in an inclusive classroom is supported by a recent research study that found that students trained in collaborative learning on computers had higher student achievement, higher self-esteem, and better attitudes toward learning than students working individually.[81] The study points out that small-group collaboration on the computer is especially effective when students have received training in the collaborative process. Students who worked in groups were found to interact more with other students, to use more appropriate learning strategies, and to persevere more on assigned instructional tasks. These findings reinforce the importance of cooperative learning activities, as part of a program of inclusive education. (See Chapter 6 for a discussion of cooperative learning.)

How does technology relate to the law?

The use of technological tools in the education of students with disabilities has been a reality even before the federal special education law. The reauthorized IDEA, however, focuses increased attention on "assistive technology." An assistive technology service is defined as "any service that directly assists an individual with a disability in the selection, acquisition, or use of an assistive technology device." Services may include the evaluation of the needs of the individual with a disability, the solution and provision of assistive technology devices, coordination of technology use with other interventions and training or technical assistance to the individual with disabilities, of professionals who work with the individual, and of family members in the use of the device(s). As with all IDEA services, assistive technology is to be provided for the child without cost to her/him or the family.

The IEP Team *must* consider the need for assistive technology devices and services as it develops the IEP for *every* student. This consideration should lead to a dramatic expansion of the role of technology, and should mitigate the limited attention given to the use of educational technology in the education of students with disabilities. The following are some of the barriers that have limited the use of technology for students with disabilities: the belief that technology was appropriate only for the more severely impaired students, special education teachers not sufficiently trained in the use of educational technology, insufficient evaluation and support devices to meet the special technology needs of students with disabilities, too few computers with alternative input-output devices, and the frequent ignoring of the needs of these students by school administrators.

As schools address the implementation of these new requirements, there are an array of federal programs that support student access to technology. These include the E-Rate program, administered by the Federal Communications Commission, that provides funds to schools and public libraries to receive discounts on telecommunication services, and several programs of the Department of Education, including providing community access (Community Technology Centers), distance learning (Star Schools Program), professional development (Preparing Tomorrow's teachers in the Use of Technology), capacity building (Technology Literacy Challenge Fund), innovation (Technology Innovation Challenge Grant Program), research (Interagency Education Research Initiative) and technical assistance (Regional Technology in Education Consortia). In most states, there are federally-funded Alliance for Technology Access (ATA) centers that provide support, training and technical assistance. Technology Innovation Challenge Grants have been awarded in 48 states; the preparing Tomorrow's Teachers to Use Technology program supports professional development activities of colleges, school districts, and state education departments; and the Technology Literacy Challenge Fund support capacity building in every state, including the purchase of hardware, software and computer applications, teacher training, and new applications of technology. (Teachers and administrators interested in learning more about funding for technology should contact their district's funded program office.)

What are "best practices" in the use of technology?

A growing body of research indicates that technology, especially the use of computers, can be used to improve what children learn and how they learn, both within school and outside it. But the mere presence of computers, or other technological tools, does not ensure their effective use. For this to occur, technology must enhance fundamental principles of learning, including active engagement of the student, participation in groups, frequent interaction and feedback, and connections to real-world contexts.[82]

The use of technology as an effective learning tool is more likely to take place when it is embedded in the broad educational activities of the classroom, rather than as an activity separate and apart from the overall instructional program as represented by the separate computer laboratory. More specifically, students trained in collaborative learning on computers in small groups had higher achievement, better self-esteem, and more positive attitudes toward learning than students working individually. Such results, according to Sivin-Kachala and Bialo (2001), were particularly pronounced for low-ability students. Students who worked in groups were found to interact more with other students, to use more appropriate learning strategies, and to persevere more on assigned instructional tasks.

Too often in the past, and especially for students with significant disabilities, the "magic" of the technology held it apart from the overall program of instruction and separated disabled students from their nondisabled peers. Increasingly, however, technology (including assistive technology) is being seen as a "diversity accommodation tool,"[83] essential to promoting IEP goals regarding inclusion, by providing access to the curriculum, peer-to-peer communication, and alternative ways to assess progress. Computers are powerful tools that can provide multi- sensory information in ways that captivate and motivate students involved in the learning process. Computers and computer-based devices can also provide easier access to text and alternate ways to write, speak, see, listen, calculate, move, and experience the world.

Beyond the modifications needed for individual students, several states have adopted policies that promote greater accessibility through use of technology. For example, Texas requires publishers who wish to sell to the state's elementary and secondary schools provide a standardized electronic version of the text for accessibility purposes. Missouri requires elementary, secondary and postsecondary schools to procure educational materials from publishers who will provide standardized electronic text. California legislation requires publishers to provide their products in electronic format for students with disabilities attending the state's public schools and community colleges.

Some general principles that apply to the use of technology that are pedagogically sound and promote inclusive practices follow:

Principles in the Use of Technology
- Select programs and software with built-in cooperative features.
- Develop peer support (or "buddy") programs, that involve classmates helping classmates. While traditionally these efforts have involved nondisabled students assisting those with disabilities, as discussed in Chapter 6, students with disabilities can play the role of helper as well.
- Ensure that the technology program for students with disabilities meshes with the school's overall technology plan. This does not mean ignoring IEP-determined assistive technology needs of students with disabilities discussed above. Rather, it ensures that those resources are incorporated within the overall school and classroom. (With the

reauthorized IDEA revoking the "incidental benefits" rule, services and equipment for students with disabilities may as well benefit nondisabled students.)

- Incorporate the use of technology as an integral part of the instructional program. Unless teachers are prepared to do this, educational technology will not fulfill its promise. The lack of appropriate technology training in preservice and in-service teacher education programs is the most commonly cited barrier to the effective use of technology in the classroom.

- Focus on professional development utilizing the collaboration between general and special education teachers, embedding use of technology in the actual teaming of the classroom.

- Provide support for teachers, in the selection, operation and maintenance of the equipment, as well as regarding infusing the use of technology in the curriculum.

- Clarify expectations at the same time as support is provided; the effective use of technology is an essential part of a quality instructional program, i.e., it is non-negotiable.

- The use of technology should not be limited to only selected subjects, activities or students.

There are a myriad of technology uses, ranging from high to low tech, across the full range of the curriculum. These include:

- some cooperative learning programs (see esp. the "Learning Together" models of Johnson and Johnson),

- texts available in various formats,

- multi-media formats to augment print presentation, as well as those with options for transformation from one medium to another (e.g., text-to-speech),

- Universal Design for Learning (UDL) material that provides presentations at multiple levels of design, complexity, and format,[84]

- word processing programs that support proper spelling, grammar, and organization,

- spreadsheets and other programs for calculations,

- tape recordings of lessons,

- books on tape,

- computer software that converts printed text into Braille or voice,

- computers that have expanded keyboards or are switch or voice activated,

- enlarged print and/or electronic enlargement devices,

- linkages to the Internet to acquire information, "visit" distant sites, communicate with persons at a distance,

- computer software that enables teachers to assess a student's mastery of material and to design appropriate instructional and curricular modifications, and
- computer software, matched to student learning styles, that enables them to master curricular goals, in a manner paced to their rhythm.
- touch screens,
- optical character recognition technology that can scan and read text aloud,
- classroom amplification and voice enhancement systems.

The ideas presented above may be used for general and special education students and range across disabilities, as instruction and class organization does. It may, however, also be useful to consider technologies for specific disability characteristics.[85] These varied and different approaches do not mean that the students should be separated one from the other, either by disability category or disabled and nondisabled. The strategies can be incorporated in an inclusive classroom, as many of them offer benefits not only for students with differing disabilities but for other students in the classroom. Teachers will find such devices familiar ones, similar to those used in everyday activities among the nondisabled , e.g., the touch screen at an ATM, an infrared device in a theater, voice recognition systems for a computer, super-titles at the opera, a taped book, etc.

Technologies for students with mild learning and behavior disorders: This group of students account for greater than half of the students with disabilities in the nation's schools, and responses to their needs often are not dissimilar from those of students "at risk." Attributes of word processing software, with ease of revising text, producing clear and readable text, and the feeling of authorship, lead to improved writing. The freeing of students from editing enables them to spend more time on the content of the writing product. Word prediction software reduces the number of keystrokes that are required to type words and provides assistance for students with spelling at various ability levels. Use of computers for communication and networking expands the learning environment beyond the walls of the classroom or the school house, and allows students with disabilities and students without disabilities to access and send information around the world. This enhanced access leads to greater learning when the student is enabled to gather a wide variety of information, exchange thoughts and ideas with others in a collaborative environment, connected through the Internet. This process goes beyond information acquisition to the more trenchant and higher order thinking involved in knowledge construction activities.

To the extent that some students are limited in their social and interpersonal skills, the anonymity of the computer is buffering. At the same time, communication technologies can foster social learning and communication skills by linking students together. As for all students, hyperlinks enable them to access a broad array of information. This is especially useful for students with mild learning disabilities in that it eases the process of making such connections. Multimedia environments provide data to students across differing formats, especially useful for those whose comfort with text is limited, as well as alternate (to print) modes of expression.

Technologies for students with speech and language disorders: Augmentative and alternative communication (AAC) devices help to make it possible for individuals with little, no, or poor speech to overcome their communication problems. Augmentative devices support/enhance speaking capability, while alternative devices replace speech as a means of communication. Some of these devices are "stand-alone," while others are computer linked. Other devices modify existing computers for use as an AAC device. For students who have difficulty with vocabulary, there are word or phrase selection devices, as well as devices using pictures and graphics. Many systems provide synthetic or digital speech output.

Technologies for students with hearing impairments: Assistive listening devices (ALD) have been in use since the 1800s[86]. In addition to the common hearing aid, mechanisms to assist students with hearing impairments include TDDs (Telecommunication Device for the Deaf), that use a keyboard to type and receive messages over the telephone and captioning that provides text for words that are spoken.[87] Other devices are: FM amplification systems, in effect a closed public address system, where the teacher, who wears a microphone, can communicate directly with the student, who wears a special hearing aid; audio loops, a variation on the FM amplification system; infrared systems, that provide better hearing in public places without wires or cords; cochlear implants, a surgically placed implant for persons with profound hearing impairments. A four disc CD-ROM set developed by Gerald Pollard contains stories frequently used by elementary, middle, and high school teachers. Appearing at the bottom of the screen are the text of the story as well as a sign language interpreter.[88]

Technologies for students with visual impairments: Large print, specialized magnification lenses (Closed Circuit Television Magnification) or electronic enlargement devices are for students with some useful vision. Optical character recognition (OCR) technology can scan and read text aloud. Earlier versions were large and bulky but more recent portable devices make them more user friendly. These devices may be useful for students with cognitive processing impairments, just as the taped recordings mentioned above are useful for those with visual impairments. Descriptive Video Services (DVS) insert a narrative description of visual elements (e.g., sets and costumes, characters physical descriptions and facial expressions) into pauses in a program's dialog. Many television sets now provide a switch that allows the user to hear the descriptive video.

The reauthorized IDEA requires that the IEP Team consider the appropriateness of instruction in Braille for all visually impaired students. The usefulness of Braille has been enhanced by the development of computer technology that reads aloud Braille text, Braille notetakers that can provide text or Braille output, and printers that can produce text from Braille.

Technologies for students with severe physical disabilities: The most common interfaces for students with severe physical disabilities are related to the flow of electrical power to a device the user wants to control. Switches can be activated by almost any part of the user's body (e.g., arm, hand, finger, chin, head, leg, or foot) or even by controlled breathing. Adaptive keyboards replace standard keys with larger ones that are easier to see and touch, rearrange the placement of keys so they are more sensitive to touch, or require less pressure to activate. Touch-sensitive screens allow the user to touch the computer screen to perform a function. Infrared sensors with pneumatic switches enable the user to operate a computer without touching it, whereby the sensor follows movement of the user's head and inhaling or exhaling through a plastic tube activates a mouse-like device. Voice recognition systems operate the computer by speaking to it.

There are both differing uses of technology based upon the nature of a student's disability and variations according to the subject matter involved. Kumar and Watson (2000) have examined the issues involved in the use of computers in science education for students with learning disabilities. They identify issues including individualizing the mode of delivery, anchoring instruction, integrating science with other subjects, and motivating students to stay on task.[89] "Transitional Mathematics Program," developed by University of Puget Sound Professor John Woodward, is designed to help middle school special education students move beyond basic math skills. It shows how to break down complex equations into smaller parts, and is available online as well as on a CD Rom, in both English and Spanish.[90]

Beyond a focus on particular disabilities or subject areas, technology devices can be viewed as interactive study tools, appropriate for all students.

These include technologies in the area of:

- organizational skills, from simple "wake-up" classes to Palm Pilot-type organizers,
- study strategies guides,
- study guides, teacher-prepared material that focus on essential knowledge and skills,
- practice quizzes, focused on particular text and other curricula material, which can be scored with teacher notification optional,
- electronic flash cards, as drill material re. basic skills,
- home-school communication,
- reference resources, across the full range of subjects,
- homework helpers, and
- hand-held tools, such as spelling check.[91]

Where can I find additional information regarding technology?

There is an ever-growing body of information both about technology in general and assistive technology in particular. Useful resources include:

Children and computer technology (Fall/Winter 2000), *The Future of Children*, 10 (2).

Gordon, D., (Ed.) (2000). *The digital classroom: How technology is changing the way we teach and learn*. Cambridge, MA: The Harvard Education Letter.

The school administrator's Handbook of essential Internet sites. (2000). Gaithersberg, MD: Aspen Publishers.

Sivin-Kachala, J. & Bialo, E.R. (2001). *2000 research report on the effectiveness of technology in schools*. (2001). Washington, DC: Software and Information Industry Association.

Teachers' tools for the 21st century: A report on teachers' use of technology. (2000). Washington, DC: US Department of Education.

More specific resources include the following:

Elias, Maurice, Friedlander, Brian & Tobias, Steven (2001). *Engaging the Resistant Child Through Computers: A Manual to Facilitate Social & Emotional Learning*, Port Chester, NY: National Professional Resources, Inc.

Hasselbring, T. S. & Glaser, C. H. W. (Fall/Winter 2000), Use of computer technology to help students with special needs, *The Future of Children*, 10(2), 102–122.

Male, M. (1998). *Technology for inclusion: Meeting the special needs of all students.*, 3rd edition. Boston: Allyn & Bacon.

Pressman, H. & Blackstone, S. (1997). Technology and inclusion: Are we asking the wrong questions? In D.K. Lipsky & A. Gartner, *Inclusion and school reform: Transforming America's classrooms* (pp. 329–352). Baltimore: Paul H. Brookes Publishing Co.

Pressman, H. & Dublin, P. (1995). *Accommodating learning styles in elementary classrooms*. New York: Harcourt, Brace, Jovanovich.

Pressman, H. & Dublin, P. (1994). *Integrating computers in your classroom*. New York: HarperCollins.

9

Additional Resources

Supporting Print and Video Materials

Available from National Professional Resources, Inc. 1-800-453-7461

Allington, Richard L. & Patricia M. Cunningham. *Schools That Work: Where all Children Read and Write.* New York: NY, Harper Collins, 1996.

Anderson, Winifred, Stephen Chitwood, & Diedre Hayden. *Negotiating the Special Education Maze.* Bethesda, MD: Woodbine House, 1997.

Armstrong, Thomas. *The Myth of the A.D.D. Child.* New York, NY: Penguin Putnam Inc., 1997.

Armstrong, Thomas. *Beyond the ADD Myth: Classroom Strategies & Techniques* (Video). Port Chester, NY: National Professional Resources, Inc, 1996.

Batshaw, Mark L. *Children with Disabilities,* 4th Edition. Baltimore, MD: Paul H. Brookes Publishing, 1997.

Beecher, Margaret. *Developing the Gifts & Talents of All Students in the Regular Classroom.* Mansfield Center, CT: Creative Learning Press, Inc., 1995.

Block, Martin E. *A Teacher's Guide to Including Students With Disabilities in Regular Physical Education.* Baltimore, MD: Paul H. Brookes Publishing, 1994.

Bocchino, Rob. *Emotional Literacy: To Be a Different Kind of Smart.* Thousand Oaks, CA: Corwin Press, 1999.

Buehler, Bruce. *What We Know . . . How We Teach—Linking Medicine & Education for the Child with Special Needs* (Video). Port Chester, NY: National Professional Resources, Inc., 1998.

Buggeman, Sally, Tom Hoerr, & Christine Wallach (Editors). *Celebrating Multiple Intelligences: Teaching for Success.* St. Louis, MO: The New City School, Inc., 1994.

Buggeman, Sally, Tom Hoerr, & Christine Wallach (Editors). *Succeeding with Multiple Intelligences: Teaching Through the Personal Inteligences.* St. Louis, MO: The New City School, Inc., 1996.

Burrello, Leonard, Carol Lashly, Edith E. Beaty. *Educating All Students Together: How School Leaders Create Unified Systems.* Thousand Oaks, CA: Corwin Press, Inc., 2001.

Bunch, Gary. *Inclusion: How To*. Toronto, Canada: Inclusion Press, 1999.

Cohen, Jonathan. *Educating Minds and Hearts: Social Emotional Learning and the Passage into Adolescence*. New York, NY: Teachers College Press, 1999.

Darling-Hammond, Linda. *The New Teacher: Meeting the Challenges* (Video). Port Chester, NY: National Professional Resources, Inc., 2000.

Darling-Hammond, Linda. *The Right To Learn: A Blueprint for Creating Schools That Work*. San Francisco, CA: Jossey-Bass Publishers, 1997.

Dover, Wendy. *The Personal Planner & Training Guide for the Para Professional* (3-ring binder). Manhattan, KS: MASTER Teacher, 1996.

Dover, Wendy. *Inclusion: The Next Step* (3-ring binder). Manhattan, KS: MASTER Teacher, 1999.

Doyle, Denis P., & Susan Dimentel. *Raising The Standard, 2nd Edition*. Thousand Oaks, CA: Corwin Press, Inc., 1999.

Downing, June E. *Including Students with Severe and Multiple Disabilities in Typical Classrooms*. Baltimore, MD: Paul H. Brookes Publishing, 1996.

Elias, Maurice, Brian Friedlander & Steven Tobias. *Engaging the Resistant Child Through Computers: A Manual to Facilitate Social & Emotional Learning*. Port Chester, NY: Dude Publishing, 2001.

Falvey, Mary A. *Inclusive and Heterogeneous Schooling: Assessment, Curriculum, and Instruction*. Baltimore, MD: Paul H Brookes Publishing, 1995.

Fisher, Douglas, Caren Sax, & Ian Pumpian. *Inclusive High Schools*. Baltimore, MD: Paul H. Brookes Publishing, 1999.

Flick, Grad L. *ADD/ADHD Behavior-Change Resource Kit*. West Nyack, NY:Center for Applied Research in Education, 1998.

Forum on Education (Producer). *Adapting Curriculum & Instruction in Inclusive Classrooms* (Video). Bloomington, IN: 1999.

Forum on Education (Producer). *Complexities of Collaboration* (Video). Bloomington, IN: 2000.

Forum on Education (Producer). *The Power of Two: Making a Difference Through Co-Teaching* (Video). Bloomington, IN: 1996.

Gardner, Howard. *The Disciplined Mind: What All Students Should Understand*. New York, NY: Simon & Schuster, 1999.

Gardner, Howard. *How Are Kids Smart?* (Video) Port Chester, NY: National Professional Resources, Inc., 1996.

Giangreco, Michael F. *Quick-Guides to Inclusion: Ideas for Educating Students with Disabilities*. Baltimore, MD: Paul H. Brookes Publishing, 1997.

Giangreco, Michael F. *Quick-Guides to Inclusion 2.* Baltimore, MD: Paul H. Brookes Publishing, 1998.

Giangreco, Michael, Chigee J. Cloninger, & Virginia Salce Iverson. *Choosing Outcomes & Accommodations for Children (COACH), 2nd Edition.* Baltimore, MD: Paul H. Brookes Publishing, 1998.

Glasser, William. *Alternative Strategies to Social Promotion* (Video). Port Chester, NY: National Professional Resources, Inc., 1998.

Goleman, Daniel. *Emotional Intelligence: Why it Can Matter More Than IQ.* New York, NY: Bantam Books, 1995.

Goleman, Daniel. *Emotional Intelligence: A New Vision for Educators* (Video). Port Chester, NY: National Professional Resources, Inc., 1996.

Goodman, Gretchen. *Inclusive Classrooms from A to Z: A Handbook for Educators.* Columbus, OH: Teachers' Publishing Group, 1996.

Guilford Press (Producer). *Assessing ADHD in the Schools* (Video). New York, NY: 1999.

Guilford Press (Producer). *Classroom Interventions for ADHD* (Video). New York, NY: 1999.

Gusman, Jo. *Multiple Intelligences and the 2nd Language Learner* (Video). Port Chester, NY: National Professional Resources, Inc., 1998.

Halvorsen, Ann T. & Thomas Neary. *Building Inclusive Schools: Tools and Strategies for Success.* Needham Heights, MA: 2001.

Hammeken, Peggy A. *Inclusion: An Essential Guide for the Para Professional.* Minnetonka, MN: Peytral Publications, 1996.

Hammeken, Peggy A. *Inclusion: 450 Strategies for Success.* Minnetonka, MN: Peytral Publications, 2000.

Harwell, Joan M. *Ready-to-Use Information & Materials for Assessing Specific Learning Disabilities, Volume I.* West Nyack, NY: Center for Applied Research in Education, 1995.

Harwell, Joan M. *Ready-to-Use Tools & Materials for Remediating Specific Learning Disabilities, Volume II.* West Nyack, NY: Center for Applied Research in Education, 1995.

Harwell, Joan M. *Ready-to-Use Learning Disability Activities Kit.* West Nyack, NY: Center for Applied Research in Education, 1993.

HBO (Producer). *Educating Peter* (Video). New York, NY: 1993.

Janney, Rachel, Martha E. Snell. *Behavioral Support.* Baltimore, MD: Paul H. Brookes Publishing Co., Inc., 2000.

Janney, Rachel, Martha E. Snell. *Modifying Schoolwork.* Baltimore, MD: Paul H. Brookes Publishing Co., Inc., 2000.

Jensen, Eric. *The Fragile Brain: What Impairs Learning and What We Can Do About It.* (Video) Port Chester, NY: National Professional Resources, Inc., 2000.

Jensen, Eric. *Practical Applications of Brain-Based Learning.* (Video) Port Chester, NY: National Professional Resources, Inc., 2000.

Jorgensen, Cheryl M. *Restructuring High Schools for All Students.* Baltimore, MD: Paul H. Brookes Publishing, 1998.

Kagan, Spencer, & Miguel. *Multiple Intelligences: The Complete MI Book.* San Clemente, CA: Kagan Cooperative Learning, 1998.

Kagan, Spencer, & Laurie. *Reaching Standards Through Cooperative Learning: Providing for ALL Learners in General Education Classrooms* (4-video series). Port Chester, NY: National Professional Resources, Inc., 1999.

Kame'enui, Edward J., & Deborah C. Simmons. *Adapting Curricular Materials, Volume 1: An Overview of Materials Adaptations—Toward Successful Inclusion of Students with Disabilities: The Architecture of Instruction.* Reston, VA: Council for Exceptional Children, 1999.

Keefe, Charlotte Hendrick. *Label-Free Learning: Supporting Learners with Disabilities.* York, ME: Stenhouse Publishers, 1996.

Kennedy, Craig H. & Douglas Fisher. *Inclusive Middle Schools.* Baltimore, MD: Paul H. Brookes Publishing, 2001.

Kennedy, Eileen. *Ready-to-Use Lessons & Activities for the Inclusive Primary Classroom.* West Nyack, NY: Center for Applied Research in Education, 1997.

Kerzner-Lipsky, Dorothy, & Alan Gartner. *Inclusion and School Reform.* Baltimore, MD: Paul H. Brookes Publishing, 1997.

Kerzner-Lipsky, Dorothy, & Alan Gartner. *Standards & Inclusion: Can We Have Both?* (Video). Port Chester, NY: National Professional Resources, Inc., 1998.

Kliewer, Christopher. *Schooling Children with Down Syndrome.* New York, NY: Teachers College Press, 1998.

Kohn, Alfie. *The Schools Our Children Deserve.* New York, NY: Houghton Mifflin Company. 1999.

Lang, Greg, & Chirs Berberich. *All Children are Special: Creating an Inclusive Classroom.* York, ME: Stenhouse Publishers, 1995.

MASTER Teacher (Producer). *Lesson Plans & Modifications for Inclusion and Collaborative Classrooms* (4-video series). Manhattan, KS: 1995.

MASTER Teacher (Producer). *Inclusion: The Next Step* (4-video series). Manhattan, KS: 1999.

MASTER Teacher (Producer). *Inclusion Video Series* (4-video series). Manhattan, KS: 1994.

MASTER Teacher (Publisher). *Lesson Plans and Modifications for Inclusion and Collaborative Classrooms* (3-ring binder). Manhattan, KS: 1995.

MASTER Teacher (Publisher). *Lesson Plans and Modifications for Inclusion and Collaborative Classrooms, Book 2* (3-ring binder). Manhattan, KS: 1996.

McGregor, Gail, R. Tumm Vogelsberg. *Inclusive Schooling Practices: Pedagogical and Research Foundations*. Baltimore, MD: Paul H. Brooks Publishing Co., Inc. 1998.

Meyen, Edward L., Glenn A. Vergason, & Richard J. Whelan. *Strategies for Teaching Exceptional Children in Inclusive Settings*. Denver, CO: Love Publishing, 1996.

Moore, Lorraine O. *Inclusion: Strategies for Working with Young Children*. Minnetonka, MN: Peytral Publications, 1997.

National Professional Resources, Inc. (Publisher*). Inclusion Times for Children and Youth with Disabilities* (Newsletter). Port Chester, NY: 2001.

Pierangelo, Roger, & Rochelle Crane. *Complete Guide to Special Education Transition Services*. West Nyack, NY: Center for Applied Research in Education, 1997.

Pierangelo, Roger. *The Special Education Teacher's Book of Lists*. West Nyack, NY: Center for Applied Research in Education, 1995.

Porter, Stephanie, et al. *Children and Youth—Assisted by Medical Technology in Educational Settings: Guidelines for Care*. Baltimore, MD: Paul H. BrookesPublishing, 1997.

Putnam, Joanne W. *Cooperative Learning and Strategies for Inclusion*. Baltimore, MD: Paul H. Brookes Publishing, 1998.

Renzulli, Joseph S. *Developing the Gifts and Talents of ALL Students: The Schoolwide Enrichment Model* (Video). Port Chester, NY: National Professional Resources, Inc., 1999.

Rief, Sandra F. *The ADD/ADHD Checklist*. Paramus, NJ: Prentice Hall, 1998.

Rief, Sandra F. *How to Reach and Teach ADD/ADHD Children*. West Nyack, NY: Center for Applied Research in Education, 1993.

Rief, Sandra F., & Julie A. Heimburge. *How to Reach & Teach All Students in the Inclusive Classroom*. West Nyack, NY: Center for Applied Research in Education, 1996.

Rief, Sandra. *ADHD—Inclusive Instruction & Collaborative Practices* (Video). Port Chester, NY: National Professional Resources, Inc., 1995.

Rief, Sandra. *How to Help Your Child Succeed in School: Strategies and Guidance for Parents of Children with ADHD and/or Learning Disabilities* (Video). Port Chester, NY: National Professional Resources, Inc., 1997.

Sapon-Shevin, Mara. *Because We Can Change the World*. Boston, MA: Allyn & Bacon, 1999.

Schumaker, Jean, & Keith Lenz. *Adapting Curricular Materials, Volume 3: Grades Six Through Eight—Adapting Language Arts, Social Studies, and Science Materials for the Inclusive Classroom.* Reston, VA: Council for Exceptional Children, 1999.

Scully, Jennifer L. *The Power of Social Skills in Character Development: Helping Diverse Learners Succeed.* Port Chester, NY: Dude Publishing, 2000.

Stirling, Diane, G. Archibald, L. McKay, S. Berg. *Character Education Connections for School, Home and Community: A Guide for Integrating Character Education.* Port Chester, NY: National Professional Resources, Inc., 2001.

Shum, Jeanne Shay. *Adapting Curricular Materials, Volume 2: Kindergarten Through Grade Five—Adapting Reading & Math Materials for the Inclusive Classroom.* Reston, VA: Council for Exceptional Children, 1999.

Snell, Martha E., Rachel Janney. *Collaborative Teaming.* Baltimore, MD: Paul H. Brookes Publishing Co., Inc., 2000.

Snell, Martha E., Rachel Janney. *Social Relationships & Peer Support.* Baltimore, MD: Paul H. Brookes Publishing Co., Inc., 2000.

Stainback, Susan, & William. *Inclusion: A Guide for Educators.* Baltimore, MD: Paul H. Brookes Publishing, 1996.

Strichart, Stephen S., Charles T. Mangrum II, & Patricia Iannuzzi. *Teaching Study Skills and Strategies to Students with Learning Disabilities, Attention Deficit Disorders, or Special Needs, 2nd Edition.* Boston, MA: Allyn & Bacon, 1998.

Teele, Sue. *Rainbows of Intelligence: Exploring How Students Learn.* Redlands, CA: Sue Teele, 1999.

Teele, Sue. *Rainbows of Intelligence: Raising Student Performance Through Multiple Intelligences* (Video). Port Chester, NY: National Professional Resources, Inc., 2000.

Thousand, Jacqueline S., Richard A. Villa, & Ann I. Nevin. *Creating Collaborative Learning: A Practical Guide to Empowering Students & Teachers.* Baltimore, MD: Paul H. Brookes Publishing, 1994.

Thurlow, Martha L., Judy L. Elliott, & James E. Ysseldyke. *Testing Students with Disabilities.* Thousand Oaks, CA: Corwin Press, 1998.

U.S. Department of Education (Publisher). *To Assure the Free Appropriate Public Education of All Children with Disabilities.* Washington, DC: 1998.

VanDover, Theresa. *A Principal's Guide to Creating a Building Climate for Inclusion* (3-ring binder). Manhattan, KS: MASTER Teacher, 1995.

Villa, Richard A., & Jacqueline S. Thousand. *Restructuring for Caring and Effective Education.* Baltimore, MD: Paul H. Brookes Publishing, 2000.

Winebrenner, Susan. *Teaching Kids with Learning Difficulties in the Regular Classroom.* Minneapolis, MN: Free Spirit Publishing, 1996.

Web Sites

No list of web sites is either complete or up-to-date. The following lists those sites of which we are aware as of Spring 2001. Many of them provide links to other sites.

Inclusion Web sites

Web site address	Self-description
www.inclusion.org	The Inclusion Network
www.inclusion.com	Best of Inclusion
www.circleofinclusion.org	Circle of inclusion
www.island.net/~bridges	Building Bridges Consulting
www.seriweb.com	Special education resources
www.asri.edu/cfsp/brochure/inclinks.htm	Inclusion links and related sites
www.caltash.gen.ca.us	Inclusion at Lenmore High School
www.kidstogether.org/	

Organizational Web Sites

www.nichcy.org	National Information Center for Children and Youth with Disabilities
www.cec.sped.org	Council for Exceptional Children
www.tash.org	TASH
www.cec.sped.org/ericec	ERIC Clearinghouse on Disabilities
www.lrp.com	LRP Publications
www.nea.org	National Education Association
www.aft.org	American Federation of Teachers
www.ascd.org	Association for Supervision and Curriculum Development
www.edweek.org	*Education Week*
www.cast.org/tools	Center for Applied Special Technology

Organizations

American Association on Mental Retardation
444 North Capital Street, NW
Washington, DC 20001
(800) 424–3688

American Speech-Language Hearing Association (ASHA)
10801 Rockville Peak
Rockville, MD 20852
(800) 638–8255

ARC of the United States
1010 Wayne Avenue
Silver Spring, MD 20910
(301) 565–3842

Association for Supervision and Curriculum Development (ASCD)
1703 N. Beauregard Street
Alexandria, VA 22311–1714
(800) 933–2723
www.ascd.org

Autism Society of America
7910 Woodmont Avenue
Bethesda, MD 20814
(800) 328–8476

Council for Exceptional Children (CEC)
1920 Association Drive
Reston, VA 20191–1589
(800) 328–0272

Exceptional Parent
555 Kinderkamack Road
Oradell, NJ 07649–1517
(201) 634–6550
www.eparent.com

Institute on Community Integration
University of Minnesota
102 Peddee Hall
150 Pillsbury Drive, SE
Minneapolis, MN 55455
(612) 624–6300

Learning Disabilities Association of America
4156 Library Road
Pittsburgh, PA 15234
(412) 341–1515

National Association of State Directors of
Special Education, Inc. (NASDSE)
1800 Diagonal Road
Suite 320
Alexandria, VA 22314
(703) 519–3800
www.nasdse.org

National Association of Elementary School Principals (NAESP)
1615 Duke Street
Alexandria, VA 22314
(800) 38-NAESP
www.naesp.org

National Association of Secondary School Principals (NASSP)
1904 Association Drive
Reston, VA 20191–1537
(703) 860–0200
www.nassp.org

National Association of the Deaf
814 Thayer Avenue
Silver Springs, MD 20910
(301) 587–1788

National Center on Educational Outcomes (NCEO)
University of Minnesota
350 Elliott Hall
75 East River Road
Minneapolis, MN 55455
(612) 624–4073

National Center for Educational Restructuring and Inclusion (NCERI)
The Graduate School and University Center,
The City University of New York
365 Fifth Avenue
New York, NY 10016
(212) 817–2095

National Center for Learning Disabilities
381 Park Avenue South
New York, NY 10016
(212) 545–7510

National Down Syndrome Congress
7000 Peachtree-Dunwood Road
Atlanta, GA 30328
(800) 232–6372

National Federation of the Blind
1800 Johnson Street
Baltimore, MD 21230
(410) 659–9314

National Information Center for Children and Youth with Disabilities (NICHCY)
PO Box 1492
Washington, DC 20013
(800) 695–0285

National Information Center for Children and Youth with Disabilities (NICHCY)
P O Box 1492
Washington, DC 20013–1492
(800) 695–0285
www.nichcy.org

National Organization on Disability (NOD)
910 16th Street, NW
Washington, DC 20006

Office of Special Education Programs (OSEP)
US Department of Education
Washington, D V 20202

Office of Educational Research and Improvement (OERI)
US Department of Education
Washington, DC 20208–5570
(202) 205–9864

Office of Special Education and Rehabilitative Services (OSERS)
US Department of Education
600 Independence Avenue, SW
Washington, DC 20202
(202) 205–9864
www.ed.gov/OFFICES/OSERS

Special Education Resource Center (SERC)
25 Industrial Park Road
Middletown, CT 06457
(860) 632–1485

Spina Bifida Association of America
4590 MacArthur Boulevard, NW
Washington, DC 20007–4226
(800) 621–3141

TASH
29 West Susquehanna Avenue
Baltimore, MD 21204
(410) 828–8274

United Cerebral Palsy Association
1660 L Street, NW
Washington, DC 20036
(800) 872–5827

Glossary of Terms

Accommodations: Changes in format, response, setting, timing, or scheduling that do not alter in a significant way what the test measures or the comparability of scores. Sometimes used interchangeably with modifications, see below.

Adaptations: a general term which in instruction refers to supplemental aids and services, and in assessment refers to accommodations and modifications.

Americans with Disabilities Act (ADA): Passed in 1990, this federal law provides civil rights protection for persons with disabilities; requires employers and businesses offering public accommodations to make them accessible to persons with disabilities; prohibits discrimination in employment; requires access in communication systems; requires schools to ensure that discrimination based upon disabilities doe not occur.

Alternate assessment: determination by the IEP Team that a student will not participate in a particular state- or district-wide assessment (or part of such an assessment). The IEP must include a statement of why that assessment is not appropriate for the child and how the child will be assessed. For such students, alternate assessments are to be used.

Attention Deficit Disorder (ADD): A condition in which a student has difficulties in directing or maintaining attention to normal tasks of learning.

Attention Deficit Hyperactivity Disorder (ADHD): A condition in which a student has significant difficulties in focusing and sustaining attention, impulsiveness, and regulation activity level.

Authentic assessment: An evaluation of a student's performance, with meaningful tasks related directly to the curriculum taught.

Behavior intervention plan (BIP): Required per the reauthorized IDEA for students whose behavior triggers special attention, per a functional behavior assessment (FBA, see below.)

Block scheduling: Scheduling for longer than the usual 45 to 50 minute periods; usually used in order to allow for the integration of curricula areas, e.g., literacy and social studies, mathematics and science, etc.

Collaboration: A team effort involving two or more adults working together and providing mutual support for each other.

Cooperative learning: A group of students with diverse skills and traits working together. This promotes collaboration, teamwork, and an appreciation of differences while fostering long-term relationships. (See Chapter 6.)

Co-teaching (or collaborative teaching): A strategy in which a general education teacher and a special education teacher plan and work together and jointly teach students in an inclusive environment. (See Chapter 4 for a description of various co-teaching models.)

Curriculum-based assessment: The evaluation of student performance per the curriculum being taught.

Differentiated instruction: An instruction system where the teacher uses various approaches to content, process, and product in recognition of learners' differing degrees of readiness, divergent interests, and learning needs. (See Chapter 5 on differentiated classrooms.)

Disability: Impairment of normal functioning.

Free Appropriate Public Education (FAPE): The guarantee per the federal law (IDEA) for all students with disabilities.

Functional assessment: The assessment of student outcomes related to living and working in the community. Usually refers to students with more significant impairments.

Functional behavior assessment (FBA): Per the reauthorized IDEA, a systematic study of a student's behavior, precedent to the development of a behavior intervention plan (BIP), see above.

General education curriculum: The curriculum per each state's requirements, for students in general. Per IDEA, mastery of this curriculum, with needed supplementary aids and services, is expected for students with disabilities. The antonym to a separate special education curriculum.

Individuals with Disabilities Education Act (IDEA): P.L. 105–17, the federal "special education" law. Reauthorized in 1997, it is the successor of P.L. 94–142, "The Education for All Handicapped Children Act," first enacted in 1975. (See Chapter 2 for a discussion of the key provisions of IDEA.)

Inclusion (inclusive education/schooling): The concept that students with disabilities, regardless of the nature and extent of their disability, should be educated with age-appropriate peers, in regular classes, with needed supplementary aids and services, in their home school. (N.B. The term does not appear in IDEA. Nor does the term "mainstreaming.")

Individualized Education Program (IEP): As required by IDEA, a written commitment on the part of the school district for the provision of services to meet the student's individual needs. The IEP includes a description of the student's current performance; measurable annual goals; required special education and related services, including needed supplementary aids and services; a description of the extent to which there is to be participation with nondisabled students; the extent to which the student is to participate in district- and statewide assessments (along with, as necessary, needed modifications); a specification of when services will begin, where they will be provided, and how long they will last; transition services needs; and measures of progress toward the attainment of the specified goals, and when and how parents will be informed of such progress. (See Chapter 3 for a description of the IEP Team.)

Information processing: The mental manipulation of symbols, words, and perceptions to acquire knowledge and solve problems.

Learning disability (LD): A handicapping condition in which a child is achieving and performing at a level that is significantly below the expectation for her/his measured intellectual ability. The discrepancy must be due to difficulties in information processing, rather than environmental or social factors.

Learning style: The way a person organizes and responds to experiences and information.

Least Restrictive Environment (LRE): The environment in which learners with disabilities can succeed, which is most similar to the environment in which nondisabled peers are educated. Students with disabilities are to be removed from the general education setting only when the nature and severity of their disability is such that education in that setting, with supplementary aids and services, cannot be achieved satisfactorily. Although the term is not used in IDEA, it expresses the concept that students with disabilities are to be educated with their nondisabled peers, supported with needed supplementary aids and services, unless otherwise and specifically justified to the contrary. In effect, there is a presumption of inclusion.

Looping: A design wherein students are taught by the same teacher(s) for longer than one year.

Modifications: Changes in the assessment that alter what the test is to measure or the comparability of scores. Sometimes used interchangeably with accommodations, see above. More broadly, sometimes used as a synonym for adaptations made in the curriculum, presentation method, or the environment to provide support for the student with disabilities.

Natural proportion: When the number of students with disabilities in an environment reflects the percentage of individuals with disabilities generally found in the community.

Natural supports: The least-intrusive supports available in the environment in which performance is being exhibited, i.e., "less is better."

Normalization: The principle that services to people with disabilities, including children and youth, should be provided with services, including education, as similar as possible to those provided to their nondisabled peers.

Portfolio: A form of assessment involving a collection of a student's work which demonstrates what the student has learned over a period of time.

Regular education classroom: The general classroom for students in a school. Per IDEA, the presumptive location for education of students with disabilities, with needed supplementary aids and services.

Related services: Those services necessary to enable the student with disabilities to benefit from special education services. Related services include audiology, counseling, early identification and assessment, certain medical services, occupational therapy, orientation and mobility services, parent counseling and training, physical therapy, psychological services, recreation, rehabilitation counseling services, school health services, social work services in schools, speech-language pathology services, and transportation. For students with disabilities, needed related services are specified on her/his IEP.

Review: The IDEA requirement that a student's IEP be periodically revisited, at least once a year ("annual review") and more extensively every three years ("triennial review").

Role release: The concept that as colleagues work together they give up ("release") their sole ownership of a particular skill or area of expertise. (See Chapter 4.)

Scaffolding: Temporary and adjustable support for the development of new skills. Once mastered, the "scaffold" is "faded or dismantled.

Section 504 (of the Rehabilitation Act of 1973): A civil rights law to prohibit discrimination on the basis of disability in programs and activities, public and private, that receive federal financial assistance.

Supplementary aids and services: Services provided on behalf of the student to implement the IEP, which may include supports for school personnel to ensure that the student benefits from special education services.

Transition services: Those services that facilitate the movement of a student with disabilities from school-level education services to subsequent services. Per IDEA, schools must begin planning this process when the student is 14 years of age.

Zero reject: The philosophy that no child, regardless of the nature and severity of the disability, should be excluded from school.

Endnotes

1 The description of the provisions of the law is based upon the Final Rules, *Federal Register*, March 12, 1999.

2 These categories and the percentage of the 5.2 million students, ages 6–21, served under IDEA, per the most recent report of the U.S. Department of Education, are specific learning disabilities (51.1%), speech or language impairments (20.1%), mental retardation (11.4%), emotional disturbance (8.6%), multiple disabilities (1.9%), hearing impairments (1.3%), orthopedic impairments (1.3%), other health impairments (3.1%), visual impairments (0.5%), autism (0.7%), deaf-blindness (0.1%), and traumatic brain injury (0.2%).

3 L. Fine (February 7, 2001), More students avoiding smaller 'special' buses, *Education Week*, 22(21), 1.

4 *Ibid.*

5 T. Lewin, Disabled win halt to notations of special arrangements on tests. *New York Times*, February 12, 2001, p. A1.

6 L. Olson, ETS to end extra-time notations for the disabled, *Education Week*, February 14, 2001, p. 5.

7 Lewin, op cit.

8 Adapted from *Improving education: The promise of inclusive schooling* (2000). Newton, MA: National Institute for Urban School Improvement, Education Development Center, Inc., pp. 6, f.

9 *Federal Register*, March 12, 1999.

10 The student *must* be invited if transition needs or services are to be discussed.

11 Cited in *A Guide to the Individualized Education Program* (July, 2000). Washington, DC: U.S. Department of Education, p. 8.

12 The material here is adapted from *Inclusion tool kit for parents: Information packet*, developed by SPAN (Statewide Parent Advocacy Network).

13 A. Hartocollis (November 22, 2000), "Teachers find toughest task is learning from each other," *New York Times* , p. B8.

14 For a wide-ranging discussion of the structure and function of teams in the middle school, see C. H. Kennedy & D. Fisher (2001), Building and using collaborative school teams, in C.H. Kennedy & D. Fisher (Eds.), *Inclusive middle schools* (pp. 27–41). Baltimore, MD: Paul H. Brookes Publishing Co. Inc.

15 S. E. Gately and F. J. Gately, Jr. (2001), Understanding coteaching components, *TEACHING Exceptional Children*, 33(4), 40–47.

16 *Ibid.*, 42.

17 The physical implication of the terms "pull out" and "push in" are contrary to the reauthorized IDEA emphasis on understanding special education as a service, not a place. Less important than where the service is provided is that the services, related and resource room, be integral with the general curriculum.

18 For a survey of such efforts, see M. F. Giangreco, P. A. Prelock, R. R. Reid, R. E. Dennis, & S. W. Edelman (2000), Roles of related services personnel in inclusive schools, in R. A. Villa & J. S. Thousand (Eds.), *Restructuring for caring and effective education: Piecing the puzzle together* (pp. 360–388). Baltimore: Paul H. Brookes Publishing Co.

19 Gately and Gately, op cit, Figures 3 and 4.

20 C. L. Wagner & M. C. Pugach, Forming partnerships around curriculum. *Educational Leadership*, 53(5), p. 62.

21 See chapter VII.

22 See chapter VIII.

23 C. A. Tomlinson & M. L. Kalbfleisch (1998). Teach me, Teach my brain: A call for differentiated classrooms. *Educational Leadership*, 56(3), 52–55.

24 See chapter VI for a full discussion of cooperative learning.

25 See chapter VIII re. the use of technology.

26 Some school districts call this "indirect support."

27 S. K. Etscheidt & L. Bartlett (1999), The IDEA amendments: A four-step approach for determining supplementary aids and services, *Exceptional Children*, 65(2), 163–174.

28 S. Cole, B. Horvath, C. Chapman, C. Deschenes, D. G. Ebeling, & J. Sprague (2000). *Adapting curriculum and instruction in the inclusive classroom: A teacher's desk reference*, 2nd ed. Bloomington, IN: The Center for School and Community Integration, Institute for the Study of Developmental Disabilities.

29 M. F. Giangreco & S. W. Edelman (1995, December). Coordinating support services in inclusive classrooms. Presentation at the TASH Conference, San Francisco.

30 S. Pavri & L. Monda-Amaya (2001), Social support in inclusive schools: Student and teacher perspectives, *Exceptional Children*, 67(3), 391–411.

31 Adapted from M. Grigal (July/August, 1998). The time-space continuum: Using natural supports in inclusive classrooms. *TEACHING Exceptional Children*, 44–51.

32 J. S. Schumm, S. Vaughn, & J. Harris (1997). Pyramid power for collaborative planning. *TEACHING Exceptional Children*, 29(6), 62–66.

33 Adapted from *Curriculum accommodations and/or modifications based on Chicago academic standards* (1997). Chicago: Chicago Public Schools.

34 B. J. Scott, M. R. Vitale, & W. G. Masten (March/April, 1998), Implementing instructional adaptations for students with disabilities in inclusive classrooms, *Remedial and Special Education*, 19(2), 106–119.

35 *Questions and answers*(2000).

36 For example, the state of Washington allows four sets of accommodations for its statewide test, Washington Assessment of Student Learning (WASL): 1. *aids*, provide English, visual, or native language dictionaries, except on reading test; physical supports and assists; isolate portion of the test;

clarify directions; 2. *scribe*, answer orally, point, use voice recognition technology, sign an answer, use a word processor, dictate to a scribe; 3. *large print or Braille*; and 4. *oral presentation* (e.g., read the math items verbatim in English). E. Johnson, K. Kimball, S. O. Brown, & D. Anderson (Winter 2001), A statewide review of the use of accommodations in large-scale, high-stakes assessments, *Exceptional Children* 67(2), 251–164.

37 C. A. Tomlinson (2001), Grading for success, *Educational Leadership*, 12–15.

38 Suggested here is a dual system: grades, one reflecting individual growth, e.g. "A" (excellent growth) through "F" (no observable growth), and the other relative standing, e.g., "1" (student is working above grade level in the subject) to "3" (student is working below grade level in the subject). Thus, a grade of B2 in science means that the student is making good growth and is working at grade level.

39 S. J. Salend (1998), *Effective mainstreaming: Creating inclusive classrooms.* Columbus, OH:Prentice Hall.

40 M. Sapon-Shevin, B. L. Ayres, & J. Duncan. Cooperative learning and inclusion. In J. S. Thousand, R. A. Villa, & A. I. Nevins (Eds.), *Creativity and collaborative learning: A practical guide to empowering students and teachers* (pp. 275–291). Baltimore: Paul H. Brookes Publishing Co.

41 S. Kagan (1989). The structural approach to cooperative learning. *Educational Leadership*, 47(4), 12–15.

42 See "Special series: Advances in peer-mediated instruction and interventions in the 21st century," *Remedial and Special Education* (January/February, 2001), 22(1), 2–47.

43 C. A. Utley (January/February, 2001), Introduction to the Special Series: Advances in Peer-Mediated Instruction and Interventions in the 21st Century, *Remedial and Special Education*, 22(1), 2.

44 L. Maheady, G. F. Harper, & B. Mallette (1991). Peer-mediated instruction: A review of potential applications for special education. *Reading, Writing and Learning Disabilities International*, 7, 75–103. C. A. Utley, S. L. Mortweet, & C. R. Greenwood (1997). Peer-mediated instruction and interventions. *Focus on Exceptional Children*, 29(5), 1–23.

45 L. Maheady, G. T. Harper, & B., Malette. (2001). Peer-mediated instruction and interventions and students with mild disabilities. *Remedial and Special Education* , 22(1), 7.

46 *Ibid.*, 7, f.

47 See also, C. R. Greenwood, C. Arreaga-Mayer, C. A. Utley, K. M. Gavin, & B. J. Terry. (2001). ClassWide Peer Tutoring learning management system. *Remedial and Special Education*, 22(1), 34–47.

48 See also, D. Fuchs, L. S. Fuchs, A. Thompson, E. Svenson, L. Yen, S. A. Otaiba, N. Yang, K. N. McMaster, K. Prentice, S. Kazdan, and L. Saenz. (2001). Peer-Assisted Learning Strategies in reading. *Remedial and Special Education*, 22(1), 15–21.

49 *Ibid.*, 8, ff.

50 B. Elbaum, S. Vaughn, M. Hughes, & S. W. Moody (1999). Grouping practices and reading outcomes for students with disabilities. *Exceptional Children*, 65(3), 399–415.

51 D. K. Lipsky and A. Gartner (1987). Capable of achievement and worthy of respect: Education of the handicapped as if they were full fledged human beings. *Exceptional Children*, 54(1), 69–76.

52 A. Gartner & D. K. Lipsky (1990). Students as instructional agents. In W. Stainback & S. Stainback (Eds.) , *Support networks for inclusive schooling: Interdependent integrated education* (pp. 81–98). Baltimore: Paul H. Brookes Publishing Co.

53 B. Burrell, S. J. Wood, T. Pikes, & C. Holliday (Jan/Feb, 2001), Student mentors and proteges learning together, *TEACHING Exceptional Children*, 33(3), 24–29.

54 W. Damon (1984). Peer education: The untapped potential. *Journal of Applied Developmental Psychology*, 5, 331–343.

55 Big kids teach little kids: What we know about cross aged tutoring. (1987). *Harvard Education Letter*, 3(2), 2.

56 A. Gartner, M. K. Kohler, F. Riessman (1971). *Children teach children: Learning through teaching.* New York: Harper & Row.

57 A. Gartner & D. K. Lipsky, *op cit.*

58 Handicapped children as tutors. (1984). Salt Lake City, UT: David O. McKay Institute of Education, Brigham Young University.

59 *National study of inclusive education* (2nd ed.) (1995). New York: National Center on Educational Restructuring and Inclusion, pp. 158, ff.

60 N. Schniewind & E. Davidson (September 2000), Differentiating cooperative learning. *Educational Leadership*, 58(1), 25.

61 It is worth noting that in the school shootings of the past several years, none of the perpetrators have been students who had been identified as disabled.

62 L. Fine (2001). IDEA doesn't hinder discipline, survey finds. *Education Week* (February 7), 6.

63 *Ibid.*

64 At the end of the chapter, we excerpt from *Prevention Research & the IDEA Discipline Provisions: A Guide for School Administrators*, transmitted by Judith E. Heumann, Assistant Secretary, Office of Special Education and Rehabilitative Services, and Kenneth Warlick, Director, Office of Special Education Programs, US Department of Education, January 2001.

65 L. M. Bambara & T. Knoster (1998). *Designing positive behavior support plans.* Washington, DC: American Association on Mental Retardation, p. 5. Reprinted with permission.

66 Excepted from L. M. Bambara & T. Knoster (1998), *Designing positive behavior support plans.* Washington, DC: American Association on Mental Retardation, Table 4. Reprinted with permission.

67 Bambara & Knoster, Table 6. Reprinted with permission.

68 Excerpted from A. Gartner & D. K. Lipsky (March 1999). *Building school capacity toward inclusive education.* A report to the Bergen County Partnership for Inclusive Education. New York: National Center on Educational Restructuring and Inclusion, pp. 42, f.

69 "How De We Measure the Impact of Positive Behavior Support?" (Summer 1999). The Positive Support Newsletter.

70 In the largest gift to a public university, $250 million has been donated to the University of Colorado to establish a center for research on technological advances that would help people with cognitive disabilities.

71 C. D. Jerald & G. F. Orlofsky, (2000). Raising the bar on school technology. *Education Week*, 19:58–108.

72 J. Lee & P. Shireley (June/July 2000), Technology access for all students. *Closing the Gap*, 19(2), 18.

73 At Help-Line, PO Box 160, 1459 Interstate Loop, Bismarck, ND 58503. (800) 265-IPAT. Book is available for $15.00.

74 Children and computer technology (Fall/Winter 2000) *The Future of Children*, 10(2).

75 *Tech-savvy: Educating girls in the new computer age.* (2000). Newton, IA: American Association of University Women.

76 M. R. Brown, K. Higgins, & K. Hartley (March/April 2001), Teachers and technology equity, *TEACHING Excetional Children*, 33(4), 32–339.

77 National Center for Education Statistics (2000). *Teachers' tools for the 21st century* . Washington, DC: Author.

78 J. Sivin-Kachala & E. R. Bialo (2000). *2000 research report on the effectiveness of technology in schools.* Washington, DC: Software and Information Industry Association.

79 W. Montgomery (March/April, 2001), Creating culturally responsive, inclusive classrooms, *TEACHING Exceptional Children*, 33(4), 4–9.

80 "Multicultural Resources" (*http://falcon.jmu.edu/~ramseyil.multipubhtml*) provides articles, reviews, and literature selections organized around specific cultural groups; "The Children's Literature Web Guide" (*http:///www.acs.ucalgary.ca/~dkbrown/lists.html*) is a rich resource for children's literature that addresses cultural differences.

81 Sivin-Kachala & Bialo, op cit.

82 J. M. Roschelle, R. D. Pea, C. M. Hoadley, D. N. Gordon, & B. M. Means (Fall/Winter 2000), Changing how and what children learn in school with computer-based technologies, *The Future of Children*, 10(2), 76–101.

83 This is the formulation of Pressman and Blackstone (1997).

84 Developed by the Center for Applied Special Technology (CAST), Peabody, MA.

85 Adapted from T. S. Hasselbring & C. H.W. Glaser (Fall/Winter 2000), Use of computer technology to help students with special needs, *The Future of Children*, 10(2), 105–116.

86 Alexander Graham Bell invented the telephone for the purpose of helping his sister, who had a hearing disability.

87 All newly manufactured television sets now must have decoders to provide closed captioning.

88 T. Gotsch (2001). Tech gains for disabled displayed on Capitol Hill. *Education Daily* (February 2), 6.

89 D. Kumar & C. L. Wilson. (2000). "Computer technology, science education, and students with Learning Disabilities," in L. Iura (Ed.), *Jossey-Bass Reader on Technology and Learning*. San Francisco: Jossey-Bass.

90 Gotsch, op cit.

91 D. Edyburn, (June/July 2000)Technology integration strategies: Interactive study tools, *Closing the Gap*, 22, 33.